War in the Trenches

The years 1914 to 1918 saw the most terrible war the world has ever known; nowhere was the horror more tragic than in the mud-filled trenches carved like scars across Belgium and France.

The book analyzes the progress of the war on the Western Front, and explains the thinking that lay behind this massive bloodbath. But, more important, the author shows in graphic detail what life was like for the soldiers in the trenches, the boredom and the bitter jokes, the sudden tension of shells and sniper fire, the deafening barrage of artillery, the constant presence of death. The battles themselves are vividly evoked, great grinding clashes fought for many months over blood-soaked ground, which killed and maimed millions of men for the gain of a few dozen yards.

The lavish use of contemporary photographs, as well as many diagrams and maps, adds visual impact to this great tragedy.

Soldiers having tea in a shell hole already partly occupied
by the grave of a comrade.

Books are to be returned on or before the last date below.

940.3

A WAYLAND SENTINEL BOOK

War in the Trenches

Matthew Holden

"Same old trenches, same old view,
  Same old rats as blooming tame,
Same old dug-outs, nothing new,
  Same old smell, the very same,
Same old bodies out in front,
  Same old *strafe* from two till four,
Same old scratching, same old 'unt,
  Same old bloody war."
(from *Gold Braid*, by A. A. Milne)

WAYLAND PUBLISHERS LONDON

More Sentinel Books

J940.3
485, 528

SBN 85340 215 9
Copyright © 1973 by Wayland (Publishers) Ltd.
101 Grays Inn Road, London WC1
Printed by Page Bros (Norwich) Ltd., England

Contents

List of Illustrations

1. How it all began

Trench warfare saw more cruelty, more terror and more barbarism than any war since the beginning of time. For four years, from 1914 to 1918, the great nations of the world went insane.

The First World War differed from all previous conflicts in the amount of power with which the armies could fight. Weapons were more deadly than ever before, and there were more of them.

Soldiers and politicians believed that the way to achieve victory was to use as much force as possible against the enemy, and so they threw all the available men into terrible battles. Countries were stripped of manpower, as more and more soldiers were drafted to the Front. Mass slaughter was inevitable.

And, with the introduction of the machine-gun, one man was given the power to kill large numbers of the enemy. One squeeze of the trigger, one burst of machine-gun fire, could mow down whole ranks of men.

More and more machine-guns were made; more and more men were pushed into battle. The spiral of slaughter soared higher. Generals and politicians lost control over events. Nations drowned in a ghastly blood bath. And nowhere was this more evident than in the dreadful trenches carved like scars across France and Belgium.

Everywhere today, there are monuments erected to those who died in the First World War – the Great War. Every town and village has a list of the men who went to fight, and who never returned. This book describes the hell they entered, and what happened when they got there.

France, 1916. British infantry soldiers struggle through the mud on the road from the trenches during the First World War.

The horror

August 1914 was an exceptionally hot month. Glorious
summer weather stretched all over Europe. And with
the heat came a war which scorched like hell itself.

In 1914, most people believed the war would soon

The horror of war. At the Battle of the Somme, 1916, Britain lost over sixty thousand of her troops. At Verdun, a year later, casualties were as bad. These skulls, army boots and helmets are a grim reminder of what the war was like.

be over. Instead, by the end of the year, it had developed into the stalemate of the trenches. Each side had a stranglehold around the other one's throat, and neither side seemed able either to win or to break loose.

Casualties mounted at a devastating rate. At the Battle of the Somme on 1st July, 1916, the British lost forty-five men killed or wounded for every minute of the battle. And this continued for a full twenty-four hours.

Whole families – fathers, brothers, sons – were killed. This newspaper item was typical: "Private Thomas Pestorisk, Scottish Rifles, has been so badly wounded that he has been invalided out of the Service . . . He is the youngest of nine brothers who joined the army, and he has lost eight brothers in the war."

Life was tragically cheap in the trenches. Dead bodies were used to build the support walls for the fortified ditches; yellowing skulls, arms, legs, could be seen packed tight into the dank black soil. Everywhere, like a pall, lingered the smell of corpses, or of the lime used to disinfect them. Soldiers trampled over dead men as they clambered along the earthworks.

Men lived daily in the presence of death. They might pass through a doorway into the underground bunker in which they slept and ate, and the doorway might be propped up by corpses, pushed there to give increased protection to those inside. There might be a pair of old boots lying in the trench – with the remains of feet still inside them. Nobody would take any notice.

Death could come suddenly, without warning, as an artillery shell exploded a man into nothing, so that no traces of his body could be found. Or death might be lingering. A man wounded in the "No Man's Land" between the lines of the two armies might have to be left to die, moaning for days among the craters.

Rats scurried everywhere, fat and well fed. According to a German soldier, "they favoured the eyeballs and the liver of the dead."

The hell

Not only soldiers were plunged into the horrors of this conflict. Women and children were also involved, and the hell spread far beyond the actual battlefields. This is one reason why the First World War is described as "total war."

For the first time on a large scale, bombs were dropped from the air. Long-range artillery wrought terrible destruction, and thousands of civilians were slaughtered or made homeless.

Each side tried to prevent food and materials from reaching the other. Shortages were made worse by the need to send as much as possible to the trenches. Materials which would normally have been used for making civilian, peace-time goods, were used instead to make ammunition, weapons and military uniforms.

In Britain, this meant that rationing had to be introduced – each person was only allowed a fixed amount of certain goods. Wheat and sugar were especially short. Butter became rare, and even margarine was considered a delicacy. Potatoes were almost unobtainable.

Prices rose. By the end of the war, a loaf of bread cost more than twice as much as it had done in 1914. Pubs were made to shut more often. Clothes were difficult to buy.

The German people suffered far worse. Loaves were made from potato peelings, ground turnips and sawdust. German children showed increasing signs of lack of proper food. "Their big heads and sunken eyes," wrote one commentator, "their faces like those of old people, their chests on which one could count every rib, their protruding bellies and rickety legs, were poor testimony to the humanity and culture of which the nations of Europe had boasted so much."

The soldiers of all nations hated the war, and could see no sense in it. The British poet and writer Edmund

Capture of a city. English soldiers marching through Cambrai in northern France. Notice the shell-damaged buildings and the crumbling masonry.

Blunden described the victim of an artillery shell: "How could the gobbets of blackening flesh, the earth-wall sotted with blood, with flesh, the eye under the duck-board, the pulpy bone, be the only answer?"

A German army doctor, Stephen Westman, asked the same question: "How could cultivated and civilized men hurl themselves against each other in this most savage manner, like mad dogs, and thrust bayonets and daggers into the chests or bellies of their adversaries?"

Suspicion and rivalry

Very few people wanted the war to take place. Nations had changed enormously during the second half of the nineteenth century. The Industrial Revolution had made them more powerful; populations grew; more food was needed to feed them; markets and materials had to be found to keep the factories busy.

The Franco-Prussian war, 1870–71. The victorious German army parades through the streets of Paris. See how sullen the French spectators look. They did not forget this humiliation and, in 1914, they were eager to avenge their honour.

The most powerful nations looked at each other suspiciously as their strength grew. Germany had emerged victorious from the Franco–Prussian war in 1870–1871, and many Frenchmen could not forget the sight of German troops marching in triumph through the streets of Paris. The 1871 peace terms had been harsh. Not only was money taken from the French as compensation, but territory as well – Alsace and most of Lorraine. The conquered provinces remained a constant thorn in French flesh.

Nations formed alliances for mutual protection: the "Entente Cordiale" between France and Britain, or the "Triple Alliance" between Germany, Austria and Italy. These alliances entangled one nation with another. Countries promised to come to the help of allies if they were threatened, or thought themselves to be threatened.

Armies grew in size and strength. Suspicions continued to fester. As one nation increased its forces, so did another to keep pace. "Arms races" resulted, for example between the Germans and the British in building massive "Dreadnought" battleships.

Politicians and statesmen tried to find a "balance of power": nations were grouped and balanced against each other. They hoped that if no nation or group became stronger than the others, then peace would be maintained. But the balance was always fragile. The generals meanwhile believed that victory would go to the side which moved the fastest, and was strongest when war broke out: an army must attack as soon as possible once the fighting had started.

This situation, based on suspicion, rivalry and fear, was extremely dangerous. It only needed a slight misunderstanding, even an accident, for a massive and all-destructive war to erupt. And if a nation felt itself threatened, it might decide to attack first. Allies would then be drawn in; widespread conflict would result – even if none of the countries concerned really wanted it to happen.

The plans

The nations of Europe were sliding towards war. Each nation began to make careful military plans, which it believed would guarantee it victory. But, in fact, these plans only served to bring the war still nearer.

Germany had the problem of having to face two possible enemies: Russia in the east and France in the west. She had too few forces to deal with them both at the same time: which way should her main armies move?

Count Schlieffen, the German army chief, considered this problem between 1897 and 1905. He finally decided that France should be dealt with first, and he created the so-called "Schlieffen Plan." A quick victory was essential, so that troops could be rushed across to the east afterwards, in time to face the Russians. The bulk of the German forces would therefore be concentrated opposite Belgium; as soon as the war began, these would stab through Belgium into France, and sweep round the rear of the French armies.

Schlieffen believed that only a few troops should be kept further south: one unit for every seven in the north. However, Moltke, who succeeded Schlieffen, considered that this was too risky and increased the number of units in the south. The chances of the plan being successful were thus lessened, since the troops striking through Belgium would be fewer in number.

Moltke, like Schlieffen and most generals of the period, believed that the increased fire-power provided by modern rifles and machine-guns made it much easier to attack than to defend. Few experts realized that in fact the opposite was true: it was very much easier now for defenders to slaughter the troops advancing towards them.

Meanwhile, the French had also been making plans. General Joffre, the army chief, laid down Plan XVII, whereby French forces would advance towards the

Above Germany prepares for war. Kaiser William and his Chief-of-Staff, General von Moltke, discuss plans for the attack on Belgium. You can only see the heads and guns of the men in front because they are standing in a trench.
Opposite above Plan of Europe at the outbreak of war in 1914.
Opposite below Map showing how Schlieffen planned to attack France through Belgium.

conquered territories of Alsace and Lorraine.

Schlieffen realized that a French advance in the south would in fact help the Germans, for they would then be able to sweep down unhindered from the north, and attack Paris and the French armies from the rear. But Moltke had watered down the Schlieffen Plan. The way was open for a giant stalemate.

Each plan was prepared in great detail. Troops would be moved by railway, so timetables were carefully worked out. But this meant that the plans could not easily be changed; once they had started to roll forward, the gigantic advancing armies could not be easily halted by politicians.

Box shows area covered by large map

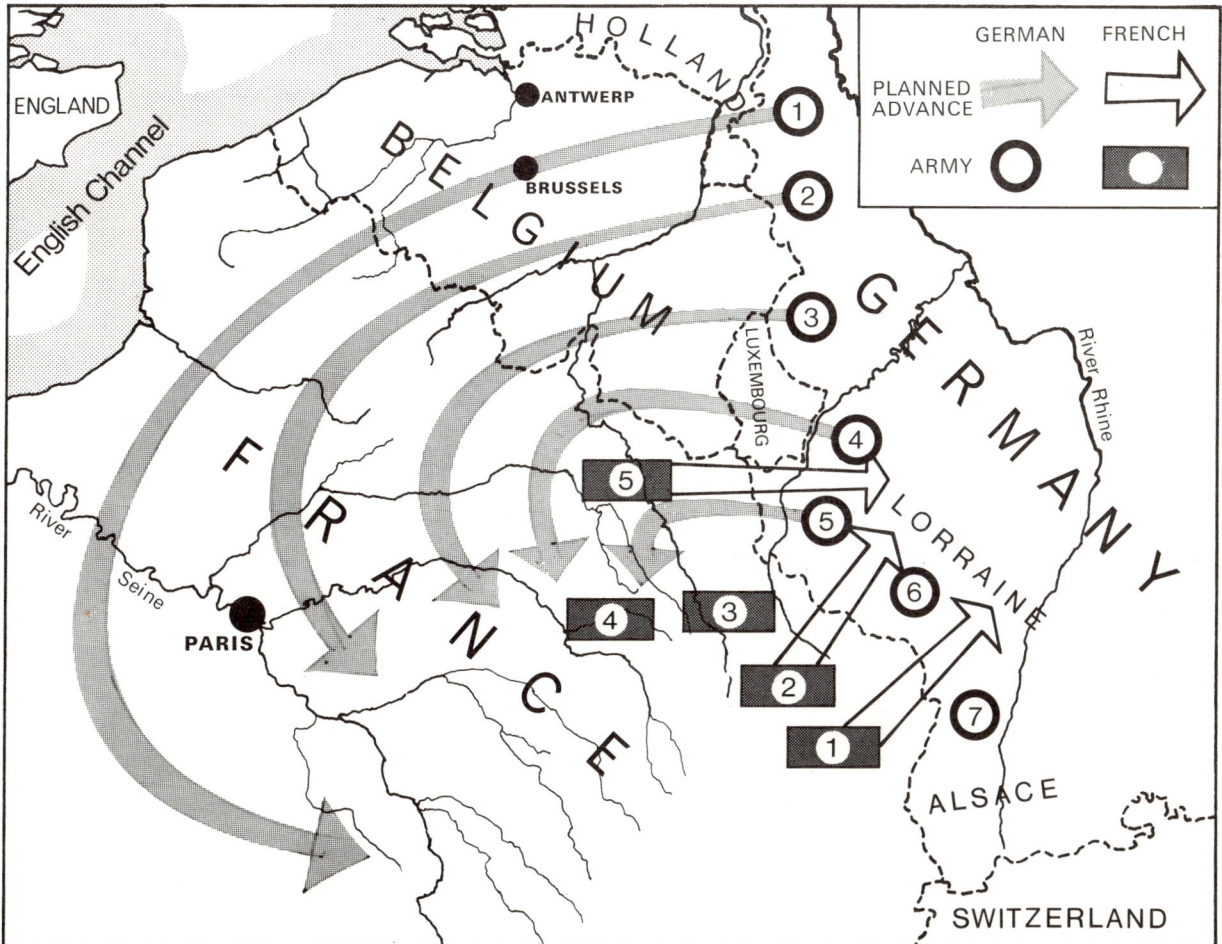

ENGLAND

English Channel

HOLLAND

ANTWERP

BRUSSELS

BELGIUM

GERMANY

LUXEMBOURG

River Rhine

FRANCE

River Seine

PARIS

LORRAINE

ALSACE

SWITZERLAND

GERMAN   FRENCH
PLANNED ADVANCE
ARMY

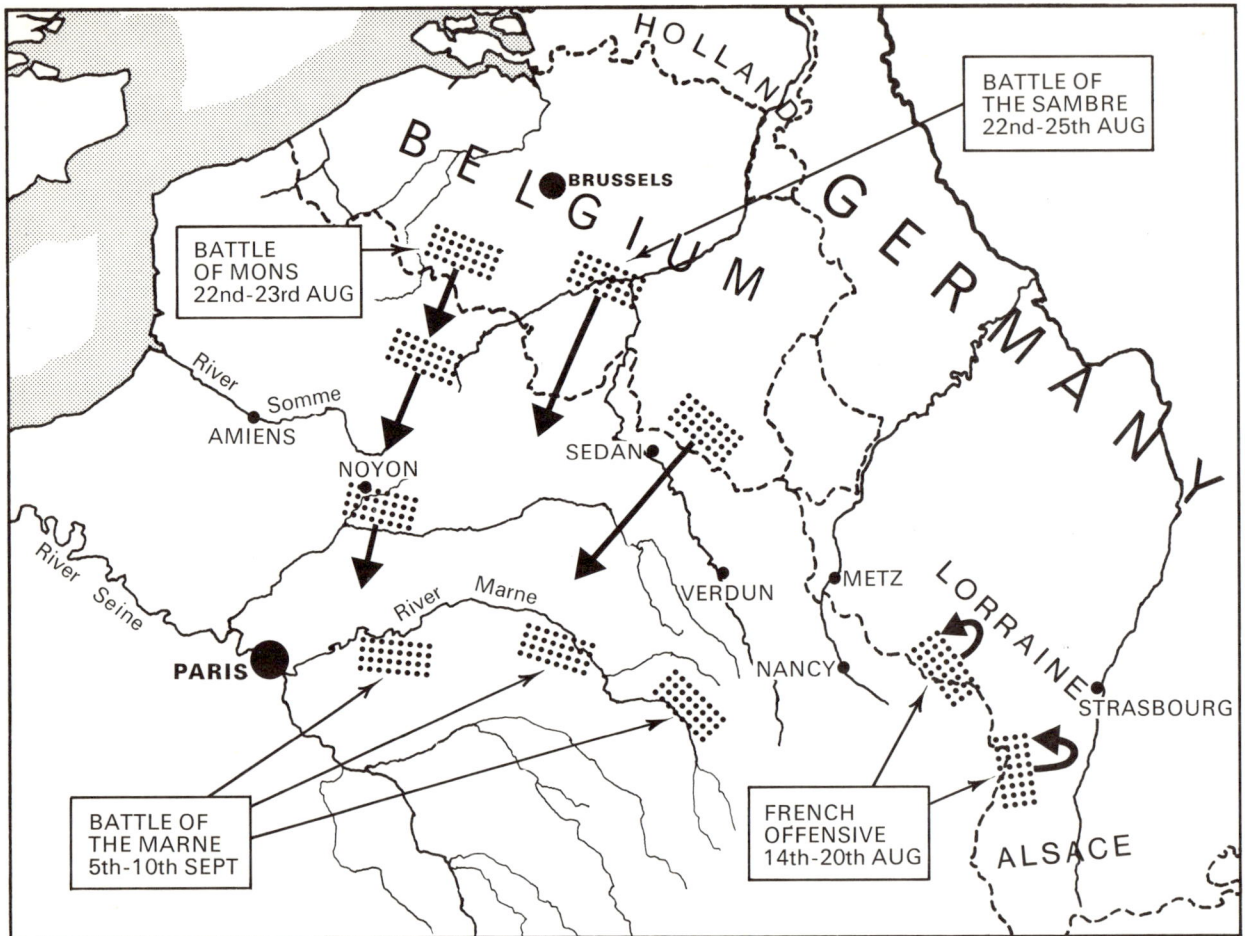

BATTLE OF
THE SAMBRE
22nd–25th AUG

BATTLE
OF MONS
22nd–23rd AUG

BATTLE OF
THE MARNE
5th–10th SEPT

FRENCH
OFFENSIVE
14th–20th AUG

HOLLAND

BELGIUM

GERMANY

BRUSSELS

River Somme
AMIENS

River Seine

NOYON

SEDAN

VERDUN

METZ

NANCY

LORRAINE

STRASBOURG

River Marne

PARIS

ALSACE

The practice

On 28th June, 1914, Archduke Franz Ferdinand, heir
to the throne of the Austrian–Hungarian Empire, was
murdered while visiting Sarajevo, capital of the small
state of Bosnia. Austria believed that Serbia, an
independent state now in Yugoslavia, had organized
the murder, and accordingly issued a stiff ultimatum.

The Serbian reply was considered inadequate.
Austria's armies started to march. Russia's did likewise.

18

Opposite Map of northern France and Belgium showing battles between French and German forces, summer 1914.

Below The eastern front. Russian troops fording a river during the Battle of Tannenberg, September 1914. Their defeat was a severe blow to Russian morale.

Germany, feeling threatened, declared war on Russia. However, under the Schlieffen Plan, France had to be attacked first. Since this attack went through neutral Belgium, Britain entered the war. And so the highly-geared machinery of war started up. Four years of slaughter had begun.

Highly-trained and efficient British troops – the British Expeditionary Force, or B.E.F. – crossed to the Continent, where it joined with French troops for the Battle of Mons (23rd August). Once again the allies were forced to retreat. The German advance continued. The Schlieffen Plan appeared to be working.

But the German army chief, Moltke, became over-confident. He believed that the French were on the verge of total defeat, and so moved a lot of his men from the west over to the east against Russia. Moreover, he ordered his forces in the south, around Nancy, to continue their advance.

The German thrust from the north was thus further weakened. The French army chief, Joffre, calmly ordered his forces to counter-attack. This resulted in the Battle of the Marne (6th September). The German command system broke down, due to the rapidity of the advance and to Moltke's lack of touch; the allies were able to hold their own.

Moltke realized that his attack had temporarily failed, and he ordered a withdrawal to a line between Noyon and Verdun. On 14th September, he was replaced by General Erich von Falkenhayn.

Meanwhile, on the eastern front, the Russians were being heavily defeated. They lost 125,000 men at the Battle of Tannenberg (26th–31st August), and the same number at the first Battle of the Masurian Lakes (9th–14th September). Russia never completely recovered.

The western front therefore increased in importance. The opposing forces however were falling into increasing stalemate, with neither side strong enough to inflict decisive defeat upon the other.

The race to the sea

The British and French allies were too weak to chase the Germans as they withdrew after the Battle of the Marne. Pursuit was delayed, and the Germans were able to build fortifications.

Both sides then tried to strike round the other by moving north. The army which struck north fastest might be able to sweep behind the enemy, and this attempt to outflank the opposing forces led to the "Race to the Sea" between 15th September and 24th November.

The race resulted in vicious clashes and, as the autumn weather set in, it ended with the Battle of the Yser, and the first Battle of Ypres. These battles in Flanders followed a pattern which was to become increasingly familiar: the clashes were long, and lasted weeks instead of days. Casualties were enormous: the B.E.F. was practically wiped out at Ypres.

Then, for ten bloody days (14th–24th December), the French and British allies tried to smash through the German lines between Nieuport and Verdun. They failed.

Now, instead of one army being able to outflank the other, both the Germans, and the British and French, had reached the far north without either side gaining the advantage. A haphazard, wavy line had been drawn across France and Belgium; on one side lay the German armies, on the other the allies.

Both sides began to dig in. Trenches and fortifications were carved across the landscape, 350 miles from the Swiss frontier to the North Sea. Millions of men and thousands of guns were put into position along this line.

Sometimes, in those early days, the opposing forces were only a few yards apart. "We occupied one side of a street," wrote a German soldier, "and the enemy the other. We climbed into lofts and fired into the rooms of houses on the opposite side of the road, or else flung

Above Reinforcements for the Belgians. The French troops are marching across fields to support their allies in the race to the sea.

Map labels: NIEUPORT, ANTWERP, FLANDERS, R. Yser, YPRES, BELGIUM, ARTOIS, PICARDY, River Somme, Hindenburg Line, GERMANY, River Aisne, VERDUN, LORRAINE, ST MIHIEL, PARIS, FRANCE, CHAMPAGNE

AREA OF TRENCH WARFARE
LINE AT START 1915
LINE AFTER RETREAT 1918

Top right The line of trench warfare across Flanders. You can see how little progress the armies made on this front between 1915 and 1918.

hand grenades through the empty holes of what had been windows.

"Part of our trench went right through a cemetery. We cleared out the contents of the family vaults, and used them to shelter us from the artillery fire; hits from heavy shells would hurl the coffins and semi-rotted corpses high into the air."

The war of movement thus became clogged into a war of the trenches. Disastrous deadlock had arrived.

2. Impact of war

How had this deadlock developed? It arose, basically, because no-one had realized that improvements in firepower – through machine-guns and modern rifles – gave greater advantage to defenders than to attackers.

The only way to inflict defeat on the enemy was to advance straight at his trenches. But machine-guns in the trenches prevented the last few hundred yards from being crossed. No matter how many men were thrown into the attack, the defenders still remained unbeaten. And so trench warfare continued.

Another mistaken belief had arisen with the development of the railways. This latest form of transport, which had been greatly improved in the years before the war, enabled men to be carried across country in far greater numbers and much faster than ever before. Supplies and ammunition could easily be sent out to them. So armies could be much bigger and much stronger.

Nations had therefore put more and more men into uniform, to take advantage of this fast new form of transport. Generals believed that the railways provided immense possibilities for the movement of massive armies.

So they did – within limits. But these massive armies could only be moved where the railway lines took them. They were tied to the railroads. Once the men had stepped down from the carriages, they had to walk, like the soldiers in the picture – and then they could go no faster than armies in previous times.

Railways could therefore deliver men quickly to the Front; but once there the troops moved slowly. And the more men there were, the more they clogged the roads and tracks. Rapid movement away from the railways was impossible.

Manpower

When the war began, most people believed that it would be "all over by Christmas." But, Christmas 1914 brought no cause for celebration. The war was clearly going to be long.

And the first weeks had also shown that the war was going to be painful. Already, terrible casualties had resulted from the clashes between these massive armies.

In the first three weeks of the war, each side suffered more than half a million men killed, wounded and captured. Never before, and never again, would so many casualties be caused in such a short space of time.

The French suffered most. Their first offensive in Alsace–Lorraine was disastrous. The butchery was dreadful. In the fighting from 21st August to 12th September, the French armies lost nearly 930,000 men – three-quarters of them in a period of less than eight days.

At the start of the war, French troops wore colourful uniforms of blue tunics and red trousers. One German soldier wrote: "Their dead, on the field of battle, made it look like a mass of poppies, intermingled with cornflowers."

The British Expeditionary Force was virtually wiped out in the first Battle of Ypres, between 30th October and 24th November. Day after day, more and more men were fed into the slaughter until bodies lay thick before the German positions.

As a result the B.E.F. was shattered. Britain's best soldiers, her pride and hope, were crumpled, mutilated and maimed.

In the first three months of fighting the British lost 85,000 men, the French 854,000. The Germans lost 677,000. These totals are the equivalent to the entire population of a medium-sized town.

As a result, each nation had to recruit more men into the army, either compulsorily or as volunteers. Younger,

Heavy casualties. The wounded British soldier being carried away on a stretcher was only one of many casualties. In the first three months of 1914, over one million soldiers were killed.

inexperienced, less well-trained men had to be sent to fill the ranks.

Britain called for help from the Commonwealth. Gallant Canadians arrived; laughing, cheeky and brave Australians; Indians, including the dreaded Ghurkas. And in Britain a new force was created – the famous "Kitchener's Army."

"Your country needs YOU." Lord Kitchener's famous slogan was more successful than anyone had expected. Half a million recruits joined up in the first month of the campaign.

Kitchener's army

Lord Kitchener was the British Secretary of State for War until June, 1916, when he drowned after his ship was struck by a mine off the Orkney Islands, Scotland. He was one of the first to see that the war would be long, and he laid plans for massive recruitment for the British Army.

The British Government was against the idea of compulsory service – conscription – which was the normal rule on the Continent. Kitchener had therefore to rely on volunteers for his new army.

Posters blossomed across Britain. "Your country needs YOU" they declared. Thousands answered the call.

Kitchener had hoped that about a hundred thousand volunteers would join in the first six months, with about another 400,000 later. Instead 500,000 men flocked forward in the first month. Thereafter the rate averaged one hundred thousand a month for eighteen months.

The pressure on men to join the army was tremendous. Posters barked at them from street walls. "There are THREE types of men. Those who hear the call and obey. Those who delay. And – THE OTHERS. To which do you belong?" "Come into the ranks and fight for your King and Country – Don't stay in the crowd and stare. You are wanted at the front. ENLIST TO-DAY."

This pressure was very hard to withstand, and those who hesitated were branded as cowards. Women would hand out white feathers to men who were not in uniform – these feathers were a symbol of cowardice.

Whole classrooms full of boys, and whole streets full of men, would go together to the recruiting offices. Special battalions were formed for the men from a certain town – for example from Sheffield or Birmingham, Barnsley or Liverpool. This system was dropped later in the war, since it meant that if the battalion was

Men outside the army recruiting office in Southwark, London in 1915. At first, there was no compulsory call-up, and the army had to rely on volunteers, like these men.

involved in a heavy battle most of the men from one part of Britain could all be killed at the same time.

Despite the mass of volunteers who came forward, some people still thought that "shirkers" were avoiding joining the army. Compulsory service was therefore introduced in 1916, which forced all single men to enrol unless they were already involved in essential civilian work.

The home front

This mass departure of men to the battlefronts was bound to have an effect back home. As more and more men became soldiers, fewer were left to undertake their normal peacetime jobs – working in offices, running trams and trains, tilling fields, manning factory benches.

Little thought had been given to this problem, for it had never arisen before. Politicians and administrators never expected so many men to volunteer.

One result of this was a change in the position of women. In the years before the war, a number of women had been demanding a better chance to earn their own living. For women were still looked upon as "second-class citizens": they could not vote, they were poorly paid when they did work, they were considered vastly inferior to men in most respects – their proper place was thought to be in the home, looking after their menfolk.

Now, with the coming of war, the women who pressed for equal rights – the suffragettes – found their demands being met. Christabel Pankhurst, one of their leaders, marched down Whitehall with a placard declaring: "We demand the right to work." This was conceded, and soon women were working in factories making shells; they became typists and office-workers – something very rare before. They went into public houses; drove trams; even became police-women. All this was very new.

Because so many men were volunteering for war, recruiting pressure had to be kept at a very high pitch so that the stream of men would carry on flowing. Politicians and women toured the country, whipping up enthusiasm by patriotic speeches. Wives and sweethearts were encouraged to urge their men into uniform.

Another way in which men were persuaded to fight was by stirring up hatred of the enemy. The Germans

Above A woman worker in the shell-casing department of a munitions (weapons) factory.
Opposite Another recruiting poster for Kitchener's Army.

were depicted as evil murderers; all kinds of stories were told of their terrible deeds. This propaganda was directed mainly at the women who, it was thought, would then push their menfolk to the recruiting offices.

They were told how the Germans slaughtered babies and refugees; how they mutilated bodies and killed without mercy. The Germans were to blame for it all. And so the war continued, in a blaze of blind fury.

Training

The total numbers of men who went out to fight – and to die – are impressive: thousands upon thousands of them were dragged into this brutal war. But in considering these total numbers, it is only too easy to forget that they were in fact made up of individual, ordinary people.

Soldiers training in the English countryside. Soon their regiment will be transferred to France; hedges and fences will become trenches and barbed wire, and enemy soldiers will return their fire.

Tom Wilkinson was one of them. For Tom, the war began while he was still at school. Like all his friends, he rushed to join up as soon as possible. And now he is starting his training as an infantryman in Kitchener's Army.

The first thing he finds is that weapons, uniforms and equipment are all in short supply. So many men are volunteering that there is not enough to go round. Nor are there enough instructors.

And so, for the moment he must make do with a wooden stick instead of a rifle, and with his ordinary clothes instead of a uniform. The day in the training camp starts at 5.30 a.m. with a tin mug of coffee and a biscuit. Then comes an hour's road running, followed by a breakfast of tinned bacon and tinned tomatoes.

The rest of the day is mostly spent in foot drill — learning endlessly how to form sections and platoons, how to advance in long lines. Bayonet drill is also important. Tom and his friends charge at sacks full of sawdust. They plunge in their sword-edged bayonets and scream "to frighten the enemy."

Only a few rifles are available for target practice, and even less ammunition. Tom has to take his turn with the others. Some attention is paid to digging trenches, but training at laying barbed wire is not attempted, since there is no barbed wire to spare.

Tom by this time has been in the army for almost a year. Soon his battalion will cross over to France. The training becomes more intense, and they are provided with proper equipment: rifle drill, firing practice, bomb throwing, trench digging, as well as battle manoeuvres, take place daily.

Had Tom joined the army later in the war, his training would have been slightly different. He would have spent less time on bayonet drill, since the bayonet had been found much less effective than the machine-gun.

31

Weapons

At the beginning of the First World War, German, British and French weapons were all very much the same.

The main infantry weapon was of course the rifle. Seventy years before, a type had been invented which was loaded at the breech, instead of down the muzzle end of the barrel, and this eventually enabled magazines to be fitted which could fire a large number of bullets in rapid succession.

The first successful machine-gun was designed in America by Richard Gatling in 1862. Its main drawback was that it needed to be wound up by hand. Sir Hiram Maxim, in 1885, brought out a version which got over this by using the "bounce-back" from the explosion to fire the next bullet. The gun would therefore fire as long as the trigger was held back and

ammunition continued to be fed into it. With slight modifications, Maxim's gun became the Lewis or the Vickers machine-gun, which was used in both World Wars.

Other defensive weapons included the Stokes mortar, which would hurl a small shell high into the air. The shell would then drop sharply into the enemy trenches. The German equivalent was the *minenwerfer*, which had a longer range and a more powerful explosive. When the weapon was fired there was a "pop", after which the missile could be seen wobbling in a high arc, before exploding in a fountain of earth, debris and bodies. Troops learnt to listen for the "pop" and watch for the missile as it approached, so that they could dive out of the way.

Bayonets were soon found to be of less value than hand-bombs or grenades. The main British grenade was the Mills. This was a great improvement on the earlier types, which had to be ignited by rubbing against a tunic sleeve or other rough surface.

The Mills grenade would fire once the priming pin had been removed. A number of seconds would elapse between the removal of the pin and the explosion, and troops learnt to delay throwing the grenade as long as possible: this avoided the chance of the missile reaching the enemy in time for the Germans to throw it back before it exploded.

Behind these infantry weapons came the huge weapons of war, the artillery, and the dreaded poisonous gas.

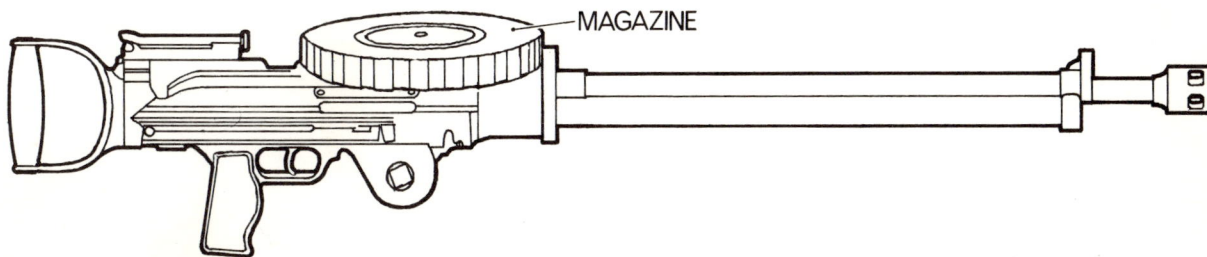

MAGAZINE

Artillery and gas

The French had the best artillery weapon in the world – the 75mm field gun. But so confident were they that they neglected their heavier guns: when the fighting began they had only about three hundred guns larger than the 75mm, while the Germans had more than three thousand.

The British equivalent to the French 75mm field gun was the 12-pounder. The German version was the 77mm, which hurled shells known to the British troops as "pip-squeaks" or "whiz-bangs."

Improvements had recently been made to shells and explosives. Dynamite had been invented in the 1860s by Alfred Nobel and cordite started to be made in the

Opposite A French 75mm field gun, one of the most effective artillery weapons of the war. Notice how it is mounted on a cement base and partly camouflaged with brushwood.

Below Gas was probably the most dangerous weapon used in the First World War. This nurse wears a gas mask to avoid the effects of the poison. Notice how the doorway is sandbagged to prevent damage from exploding shells.

1890s. Smokeless powder had also been adopted, which made it harder to see where a gun was firing from – and which ended the previous thick covering of smoke which obliterated battlefields.

Now these battlefields could be covered on purpose with special smoke from other shells, designed to hide attacking troops from the enemy. Or battles could be covered with something far more terrible – poisonous gas.

The French were the first to use gas in the war, by firing tear-gas grenades in August, 1914. The Germans followed with far more ruthlessness.

After experimenting with a rather ineffective chemical against the British in October, 1914, they opened five hundred cylinders of chlorine gas against the French in April of the following year. The gas, escaping from the containers, blew across the French lines for a distance of four miles. French soldiers lay strewn on the ground, coughing and choking as they breathed the chlorine. The Germans made full use of the panic, and the French suffered over fifteen thousand casualties.

Both sides started to use chlorine on a large scale. Another chemical, phosgene, was employed in an attempt to seep through the crude gas masks then being worn. The Germans also hurled vomiting gases: these made men take off their gas masks to be sick, after which they would be attacked by other chemicals.

But by far the most terrible chemical was "mustard" gas, which was first used by the Germans at Ypres in July, 1917. Gas masks gave little protection, because the liquid penetrated clothing to cause severe burns, and huge festering blisters. Even today there is no adequate treatment for mustard gas wounds.

3. At the Front

Massive artillery shells, machine-gun and rifle fire, mines, gas – all this meant that the chances of survival for boys like Tom Wilkinson were extremely slim.

In 1915 an average of 19,000 British soldiers were killed each month. By 1916 this had risen to 44,000, to 56,000 in 1917 – and to a ghastly 75,000 in 1918. More British soldiers were therefore slaughtered in the single year of 1918 than the Americans have lost so far during the whole Vietnam war.

Tom, crossing the Channel on a crowded troopship, is sure that he will be one of the lucky survivors. Most men thought the same.

He lands at Boulogne and spends some days at the famous military school in Harfleur, known as the "Bull Ring." He then boards a jammed troop-train for the journey to the Front. Men are loaded into cattle-trucks, which have crude notices painted on the side: "Forty men or eight horses."

Onward goes the train across the flat French countryside, jerking and creaking on the tracks through the lines of silver poplar trees and lush green meadows. War still seems many miles away.

And then the rumbling wheels screech to a halt for the last time. Tom can hear a thin French voice calling out the name of the station. He jumps down from the train – and sees the railway lines beyond the station overgrown with weeds. The tracks are split. Twisted, they point to the sky. Tom has reached the end of the line.

Up roll a number of grey-painted buses, taken from the streets of London and shipped to France for transport vehicles. And so Tom arrives at the battalion's base camp.

The trenches are still six miles away. But that night he sees war for the first time: the night sky is lit to the east by intermittent flashes, like distant summer

The way to the Front. Of the thousands of men who went to the trenches, very few returned unscathed. lightning, and he hears the deep grumbling of guns, like thunder.

The trenches

By the time Tom Wilkinson arrived in France, early in 1916, the trench system was almost fully developed. The armies had had many months to get used to this new kind of warfare.

To begin with, the fortifications merely made use of existing farm ditches, walls and dips in the ground. Very soon, however, trenches became deeper and

Below Front-line trenches. A soldier loads a mortar outside a heavily sandbagged trench on the Verdun front, France 1916.

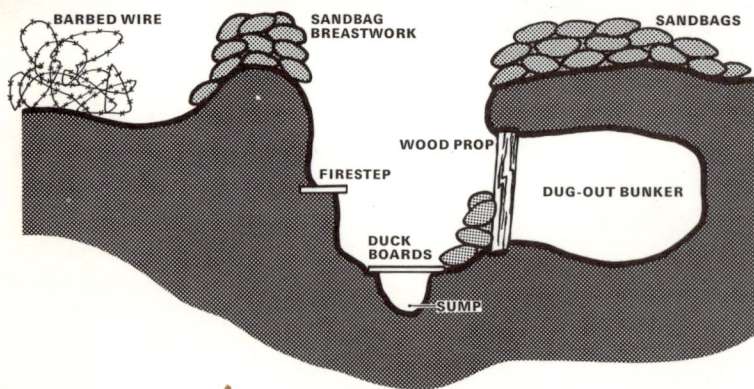

BARBED WIRE   SANDBAG BREASTWORK   SANDBAGS

WOOD PROP

FIRESTEP   DUG-OUT BUNKER

DUCK BOARDS

SUMP

Left Diagrammatic section showing how a trench was made. The bunkers served as quarters for the men not on duty.

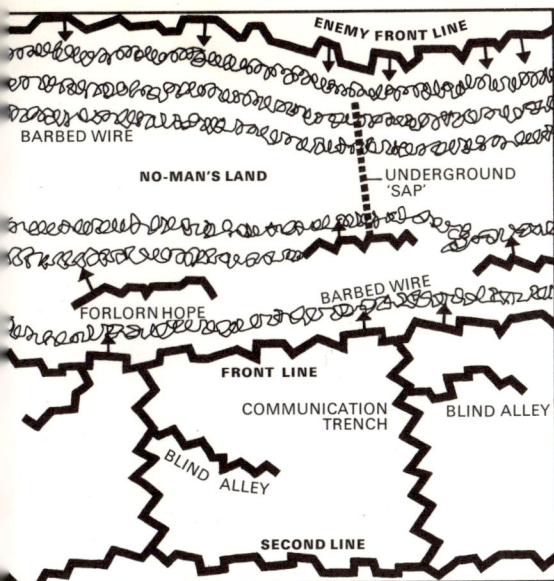

Aerial diagram showing the lines of trenches of two opposing armies. Each trench was made to zig-zag, so that an enemy could not cause heavy casualties by firing straight along it.

stronger. They straggled across the countryside in a haphazard fashion, merely following the lines of the confused fighting of 1915. Some areas protruded out into enemy territory – these were called salients. Many lives were lost trying to get rid of them, and to straighten the trench lines.

Trenches were built more than six feet deep, with ledges for soldiers to stand on to fire over the top. Each trench was dug in a zig-zag fashion – this prevented the enemy from being able to fire down the whole length of the trench system. Blind-alleys were constructed to confuse the enemy, in case of a successful German advance.

Underground bunkers or dug-outs served as head-quarter rooms, and as eating and sleeping places for a fortunate few. Boards were laid along the bottom of the trenches, with holes dug underneath in an attempt to drain away water. But the smell was always horrible: rotting bodies, sweat, cordite, dank earth and sickly disinfectant vied with each other.

Communication slits ran from the front line to the trenches at the rear. And, in the "No Man's Land" between the British and German lines, there were "Forlorn Hope" positions: shallow dug-outs into which men would crawl during the night, to stay there throughout the next day.

Sandbags were used to strengthen the trench walls and provide a breast-work in the front. The sides of the trench were shored up with wood. From the forward trenches ran underground passages or "saps" – used in an attempt to make mines blow up as near as possible to the enemy lines. Listening devices there would pick up the sounds of digging, and the moment of greatest danger was when the digging sounds stopped. That meant that a mine was about to explode.

This then, was "home", for Tom Wilkinson, and for thousands of others like him – British, French and German.

Trench life

Tom stays at the base camp, behind the trenches, for a week. He then starts the usual breaking-in system of spending a night or two in the trenches to get used to them, and returning to base during the day.

The time then comes for Tom to do a full turn of duty in the trenches. Like most soldiers, he finds that he becomes used to the routine of trench life surprisingly quickly. He is lucky – the war is comparatively quiet for the moment.

But, although no big battles are taking place, Tom soon becomes accustomed to the sight of dead bodies. The first time he sees a dead man he gazes at the corpse with wonder. Now, every morning, he wakes up to see new bodies shrouded in shapeless blankets, victims of fresh sniper fire.

At dawn each day, the whole battalion assembles ready for a possible attack in the misty, murky half-light. If no attack has emerged from the enemy lines by full daylight, the men begin the day's routine.

Company commanders report the results of the night's patrols; snipers keep watch from the positions they have taken up during the darkness; thick tea is brewed and the men fry tinned bacon. Sometimes Tom can catch the smell of German breakfasts wafting across from the enemy trenches.

Men write letters, or fill in field postcards which have simple sentences printed on them: "I am well and unwounded" or "I am wounded but recovering." The soldier merely underlines the right sentence.

Three rifle inspections are held each day. And, throughout the day, there is the sporadic whistling, shattering crunch of shells. Rifles crack constantly like paper bags being burst. A man who carelessly pokes his head above the soil risks instant death from German snipers.

Even in the moments of calm, death broods sullenly

To thousands of soldiers, the trenches were "home" for months at a time. This British soldier gets on with the day's routine, watched by his superior officer.

Right For many, the trenches were not only "home" but the "end of the road." For these German soldiers, photographed after the battle of Cambrai, 1917, the war is over. Death was a frequent visitor to the trenches.

over the battlefields. Men talk and joke, but death is always just around the corner. And the filth is constantly with them: the men are covered with lice and bugs.

Some troops suffer from "trench feet" caused by the damp. They lose all sense of feeling in their feet, and the treatment includes pricking them deep with a needle to see just how far the lack of feeling goes.

The daily routine

Tom squats over a tiny stove and cooks his lunch – the usual bully-beef and bread. He prefers to cook his own food, rather than share in one of the enormous stews, which have great gobbets of grey fat floating on the scummy surface.

He tosses away half his bread: this is brought to the troops from the rear each night and, the previous night, the carrier had come under fire as often happens, and had dropped his burden into a pool of water which was

Opposite A field kitchen, 1916. Looking at this primitive machine, bogged down in the thick mud, it is not surprising that soldiers in the trenches preferred to cook their own food.

Below Off-duty in the front line, 1916. Although, for a short time, these soldiers could smoke and chat, they always had to be on the alert for enemy shells.

shared by a rotting corpse. Tom can still taste the bitterness.

He gossips for a while with friends. "Got any peace talk?" asks a soldier, on hearing that Tom has just come from home. Another one says: "Haven't you heard? The British army will soon be going home – all of us in one rowing boat!"

The men talk about their commanders, General Sir John French and later Field Marshal Haig, without knowing anything about them – indeed, the troops know very little about the war, except what is happening in their own small trench areas.

The gossip ends abruptly. Shrapnel shells burst overhead just down the trench. Screams pierce the noise of the explosion. Tom feels a rush of hot air as the blast reaches round the corner, and he sees clouds of evil green smoke billowing suddenly upwards.

He shivers as he lies in the slimy mud at the bottom of the trench. "Don't fret, don't fret," says an experienced soldier. "Just lie still." The explosions die away.

The talking starts up again. Three men have been blown to pieces only a few yards away, and two of them were brothers. But the men continue to gossip as if nothing had happened.

Later on, Tom sneaks a look through the loop-hole at the enemy lines. He can hear a German soldier playing a flute in the trench opposite, wiling away the time. A fair-haired German boy carries a mess tin; dogs run across the beaten soil behind the enemy lines; a group of men are filing through a wrecked clump of trees. British shrapnel sends them all scurrying to cover.

Just before tea, British troops line the trench walls. They suddenly climb onto the fire-step and blast off their weapons. The Germans reply. Then, the firing ceases. And, as evening comes, Tom can still hear the flute player across in the German lines.

Night in the trenches

Night falls, and with it come artillery shells. Tom crouches, huddled and trembling, in the damp darkness of the trench. The noise is ear-shattering – whining and whistling shells, violent eruptions, screams, calls of "stretcher, stretcher."

The sky is lit with sparks, spitting blue, red and yellow. Strips of shrapnel, red hot, split the black firmament. Signal rockets swoop upwards, and flares dangle on parachutes, giving forth an eerie glare.

The barrage ends. Tom stops trembling. Ten men from his company have been killed.

Later on, he takes his turn at sentry-watch. He peers into the black in front of him through the tangled barbed wire. Shadows seem to move. A rifle cracks just down the line – Tom jumps with the sudden shock, but finds that it was only a soldier rat-shooting: this, a favourite sport, involves sticking a piece of meat on the end of a bayonet and, when a rat comes to take the bait, pulling the trigger.

Tom ends his sentry-duty and tries to sleep. He lies in the bottom of the trench, wrapped in his greatcoat. This is the only place available, but the men walking down the trench keep blundering into him in the dark.

Two men, an officer and a soldier, slip out of the trench into "No Man's Land" for the start of a patrol. One sentry whispers to another: "Patrol going out," and they disappear soundlessly into the night, their faces smeared with mud. A flare rises from the German lines soon after they have gone; no rifle shots sound, so they must have escaped detection.

Sometimes a patrol might be unable to return before dawn. The men then have to hide in one of the many shell-holes, sharing it with the remains of the dead, until darkness falls again.

Other men venture out at night to find a position from which they can snipe at the enemy the next day.

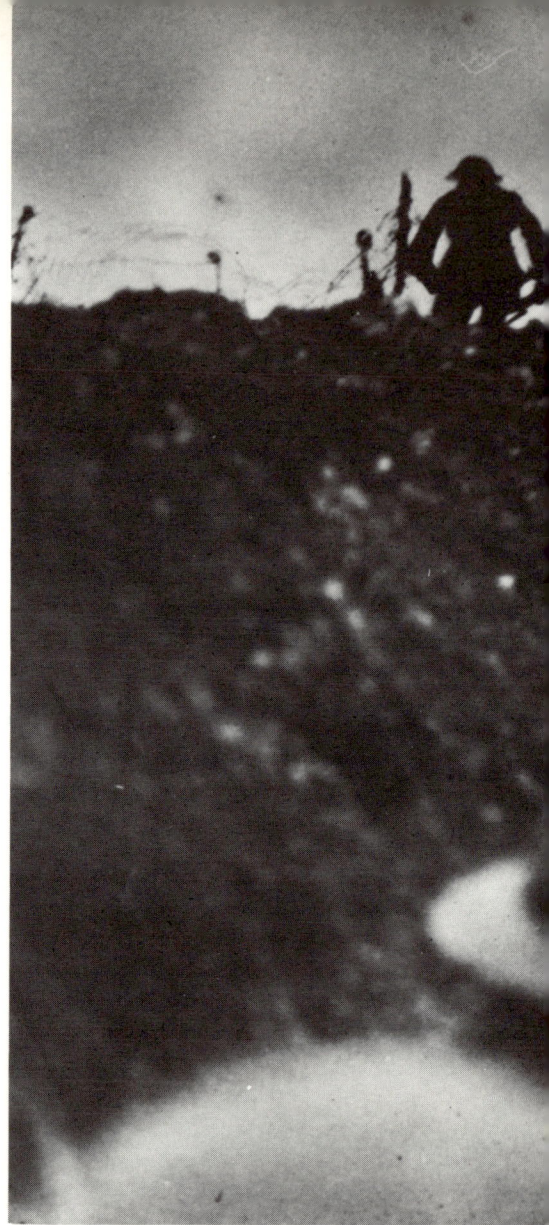

Night attack. As British troops go over the top of the trenches, the sky is lit by German artillery fire.

Theirs is a lonely duty. They have to stay in hiding until an enemy soldier shows himself, perhaps only for a split second; they fire, then scuttle away again to another hole.

All these tasks – sniper duty, patrolling, raiding, or merely staying in the trenches – are full of danger. Life is short, even without the big battles.

From the German side

Life is no easier and no safer for the Germans. Many of them too, are only just out of school. One of these boy soldiers is called Erich. His trench is just opposite Tom's. Erich didn't want to fight in a war; he feels no hatred for the British, and cannot understand why they wish to wage war against Germany.

Erich's daily routine is much the same as Tom's. His trenches are slightly deeper and better protected, but friends are still being killed and he still lives in constant danger. He is also subjected to stricter discipline than Tom: he knows, for example, that even if he is wounded and in a hospital bed he must "lie to attention" if a senior officer approaches, no matter what pain he may be suffering.

His food is not much better than that served in the English trenches: mainly noodle soup, with cow meat as tough as rubber, and stiff black rye bread. Sometimes he spreads "Hindenburg fat" on his bread – this is nicknamed after the German military leader, and is in

fact nothing more than turnip paste.

Erich's unit is considered a good one, and he wears the famous spiked helmet, the *pickel haube*. This helmet was designed to ward off sword strokes and is quite useless against shell splinters and bullets.

His colleagues include some skilled snipers. The Germans generally have better snipers than the British, and they use telescopic sights. They can hit a British cap badge at enormous range.

Tom often feels that the Germans are strong and almost unbeatable. Yet Erich thinks the same thing about the British. Here is a German description of one desperate British attack. "A series of extended lines of infantry were seen moving forward from the British trenches. They came on at a easy steady pace."

The Germans opened fire. "All along the line, men could be seen throwing up their arms and collapsing... Men, badly wounded, rolled about in agony. The British soldier, however, does not lack courage. The extended lines, though badly shaken and with many gaps, now came on all the faster... Again and again they broke against the German defences like waves against a cliff, only to be beaten back."

Above Behind the German lines. Doctors attend the wounded at a first aid post during the Arras offensive. Notice the blood stain spreading from the soldier's leg wound.

Opposite German army cooks preparing a meal for their troops in an occupied French farmhouse near Verdun.

Right The spiked *pickel haube* helmet, worn by German troops during the First World War. It was designed as protection against sword strokes, and was not much use in a war of long-range firearms!

Relief and rest

Both British and German battalions usually stay in the front-line trenches for about two weeks before they are relieved by another unit. Sometimes, if men are in short supply, a unit might not be relieved for a month or more. Then men will collapse under the strain, sentries fall asleep while walking.

Erich and Tom are relieved at about the same time.

Opposite Behind the lines life continues much as usual. Crops have to be harvested despite the fighting. Soldiers resting at the base camp noticed the contrast with the Front.

Above Leave or no leave, training for war has to continue. These British troops practise an attack from mock trenches before going back to the real thing.

Wearily, they crawl away from one another, through their communication trenches, to the rear lines. Battalions are switched at night, to prevent the enemy from taking advantage of the temporary upheaval.

When dawn breaks, both Erich and Tom can note the contrast between the rear lines and the Front. Here, the air is sweet and fresh. Fields of untouched corn wave in the breeze. Birds sing. Poplar trees stand upright. Streams run clean and clear, and glittering minnows dart under the banks.

Yet, only a few miles behind them, the earth has been churned into stinking mud; trees are twisted into jagged black skeletons; everywhere there is the stench of death.

Tom settles into his base camp. He enjoys swimming in the nearby river and washes away some of the trench filth – but the grime still remains deep embedded in his skin. He lies in the field and feels the warmth of the sun on his pallid yellow face.

The soldiers enjoy better food in their base camp. Tom also enjoys an occasional visit from a popular entertainer, who has come out from Britain. But these visits are rare; more often, the troops have to find their own amusement. Men bawl out the songs – "Take me back to dear old Blighty" and especially "It's a long way to Tipperary."

But life is not all rest. Tom's battalion, like Erich's on the far side of the trenches, is kept hard at work. The men have to sweat across the fields, attacking mock enemy positions and humping their equipment over long distances. Tom has to carry a large pack, a small haversack, his water bottle, rations, gas mask, ammunition, greatcoat, groundsheet, spade, rifle and bayonet – all this weighs sixty-six pounds.

At any moment he might have to return to the Front. And even the relief areas are within range of the enemy's heavy artillery.

c

Blighty and Berlin

Real rest and safety can only be obtained by going home to Britain – which the troops call "Blighty" – or, for Erich, to Berlin.

Tom and Erich are each told they can go home for a brief leave. Excited, they board the crowded, uncomfortable troop-trains and head away from each other and from the battlefields.

Tom jostles and pushes his way onto a troopship, crosses the Channel and arrives in London. Everywhere, he sees men in uniform. Squads of Military Police are on constant watch – these policemen can send any man they see misbehaving straight back to the Front. Even officers are inspected to make sure they are smart enough.

Tom reaches the Kentish village where he lives, and is welcomed home by his mother and father. But he finds that people generally do not make a great fuss of him: so many men from his village are in uniform, so many of them have been killed or wounded, that his arrival is commonplace.

He reads the newspapers, and finds the reports they contain very inaccurate. Headlines declare: "British Advance Unresisted" and "Victory this Year, says Haig." This seems a far cry from what Tom himself has experienced. He also notices that prices have risen drastically.

Erich, too, is finding many changes. Like Tom, he has a difficult journey home. His train is stopped on the German frontier; all the men have to strip and be cleansed of lice. Their hair is hacked down to a stubble, and they are steeped in a tub of evil-smelling disinfectant. It hardly seems to Erich that this is the way to treat "homecoming heroes."

In Berlin, as well, the Military Police are everywhere. Erich goes to the Royal Opera House, and is arrested because his gloves are not according to regulations.

Scene in a German street during the First World War. Notice that the cart is being pulled by oxen, since all the horses have been taken over for use by the army.

Right English propaganda posters put up during the First World War to discourage waste of any kind.

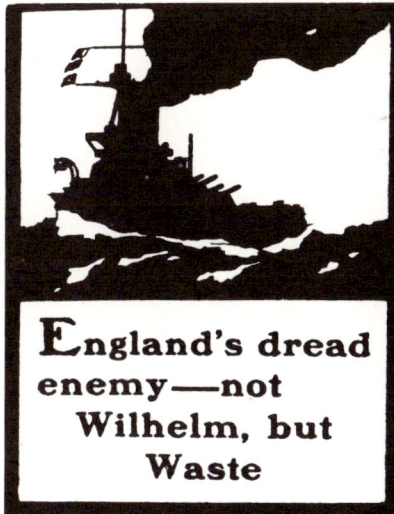

England's dread enemy—not Wilhelm, but Waste

An ounce of food saved now is worth a pound at harvest time

England's enemies, Huns, hoarders, and heedless housewives

Save your Food, Save your Country!

German prices are even higher than those in Britain. Women wear shabby, much-mended dresses, mostly in black because they are mourning for their dead.

Tom and Erich experience the same, unexpected feeling: after a few days, they want to go back to the Front, despite all their fears. They find themselves out of place: they feel dirty and lonely; their beds are too soft. Home is no longer home. They want to be back with their friends – even though great and terrible battles are approaching.

4. The battles

Other arenas of war saw vicious fighting between 1914 and 1918, apart from the trenches in France and Belgium. But the Western Front, with its line upon line of trenches, was seen as the most important. Here, believed the politicians and the generals, would the war be won or lost.

Trenches became fixed in 1915; both sides were in strongly protected positions. The result was stalemate and stagnation. Yet, despite the strength of German defence, the British and French allies constantly attempted to break through the enemy lines. The result was horrible slaughter. Generals and politicians made cold-blooded calculations as to how long it would take before the entire manhood of their nations was wiped out.

The battles were endless trials of strength, which lasted for many months and killed or maimed literally millions of men. Attacks were started by massive artillery bombardments, sometimes lasting several days. The idea was to batter the enemy trenches, to exhaust the opposing troops, and to cut through their barbed wire and communication lines. Hundreds and thousands of shells were rained down. The noise was tremendous. The bombardment would continue for hour after deafening hour, through night and day.

Then the infantry troops would emerge from their trenches, hidden perhaps behind a smoke screen. Men would form into long lines and move forward in waves at a gentle walking pace. Often the artillery barrage would still continue, landing shells just in front of the advancing men, clearing a path·for them. And they walked on towards the enemy trenches. . .

The havoc of heavy artillery as a German shell explodes near Verdun.

Steps to stalemate

The year 1915 saw a gradual move towards stronger and deeper trenches.

Early in the year the French, commanded by Joffre, attempted to free areas under German control in the French districts of Artois and Champagne. The attempts largely failed. The Germans counter-attacked

Aftermath of battle. A British military policeman escorts a wounded German prisoner, captured at the battle of Ancre, 1916. Notice the capes and round, peaked *képis* of the French soldiers in the background.

and, between the beginning of January and the end of March, horrific casualties were suffered by both sides in a useless effort to gain a few miles.

A German boy, perhaps like Erich, described his part in a counter-attack near La Bassé Canal. "At noon we went over the top. After storming less than a hundred yards, we ran against an almost concrete wall of whistling and whining rifle and machine-gun bullets.

"My company commander had his face shot away; another man, yelling and whimpering, held his hands to his belly and, through his fingers, his stomach protruded. . . . A young boy cried for his mother, bright red blood spurting out from his face.

"I flung myself into a shallow shell-hole, half filled with muddy water, and here I found four other chaps, two of them wounded. The water slowly became red. . . . No fewer than 960 young men had been killed, and this just to gratify the whim of an irresponsible and over-ambitious general."

Unfortunately, such whims were to become increasingly common, on both sides, as generals attempted to "tidy-up" the trench lines by winning over tiny areas of ground.

Autumn saw another inconclusive offensive in Artois and Champagne. The British then tried to break through at Loos. An eye-witness described this British advance. "The drizzle of rain had cleared, leaving a thin mist, when at 6.30 a.m. the infantry clambered out of their trenches, and in the fog of gas and smoke, began to advance across 'No Man's Land.' They were in fighting dress – without greatcoat and pack – but cumbered with bombs, picks and shovels and extra rations.

"All ranks wore the original pattern smoke helmet – a flannel bag – over their faces. . . . With the front down, they could hardly see through the talc-covered eye-holes."

The attack caused further terrible casualties, far greater than the gain in ground could possibly justify.

1916 – Verdun

Both the French and the German commanders, Joffre and Falkenhayn, planned massive attacks to break the trench deadlock. But the Germans struck first, on 21st February, 1916.

Falkenhayn's troops aimed at the Verdun region. The attack was launched over an area eight miles wide, and started well. But Joffre was determined that Verdun should not be lost. He ordered all possible men into the defence, commanded by General Pétain, and the German advance was painfully halted.

The Germans pushed again on 6th March, aiming at the same area. For the rest of the month, a series of attacks and counter-attacks left the sodden, blood-stained ground heaped high with mangled corpses. Pétain's motto was adopted by the French army for the rest of the war: "*Ils ne passeront pas!*" – "They shall not pass!"

German shells exploded in the rear of the French

Left Plan of the battle of Verdun, 1916. By the time the French had beaten back the Germans, nearly a million soldiers had been killed.

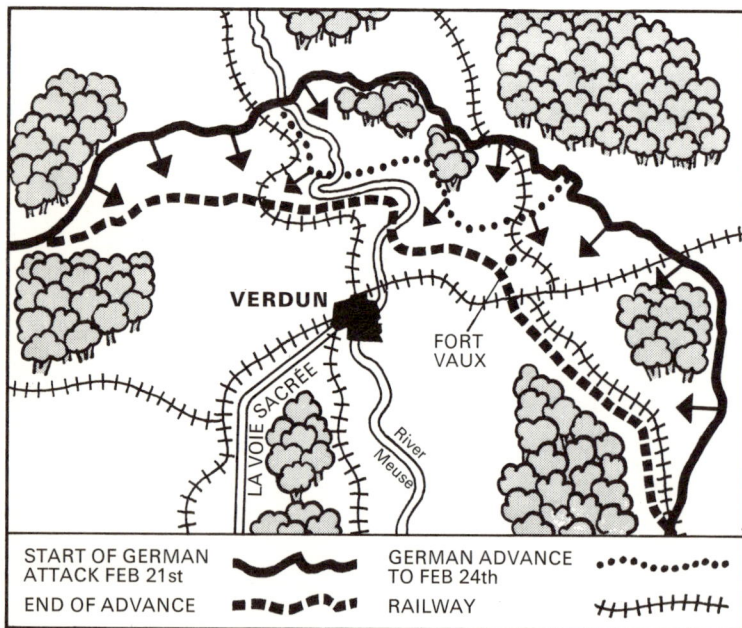

START OF GERMAN ATTACK FEB 21st	GERMAN ADVANCE TO FEB 24th
END OF ADVANCE	RAILWAY

VERDUN

FORT VAUX

LA VOIE SACRÉE

River Meuse

Above French troops shelter by the fortress of Verdun. The man standing behind the table is entertaining his comrades by playing the fiddle.

forces, and slashed the supply lines to the Front. Only one road was left, nicknamed by the French "*La Voie Sacrée*" – "The Sacred Way." Trucks were blown to pieces; waggons and bleeding horses were left scattered across the battered track. But road gangs constantly repaired the shell craters, despite high casualties, and the track remained open. Once more, the Germans were held.

And once more the Germans attacked, on 9th April. It was a long battle. The French line in the western part of the area was almost broken in early July. But troops clung to their positions. On many days there seemed to be more dead soldiers in the trenches than those still alive. Rifles became red-hot to the touch from all the firing. Machine-guns almost melted. Men became crazy from shell-shock and fear. But the French still resisted.

At last, the Germans were forced to take men from the Verdun area to fight in the east against the Russians. Falkenhayn was relieved of his command on 29th August, to be replaced by a partnership of Hindenburg and Ludendorff. These two generals decided to cut their losses and to move onto the defensive.

The French themselves attacked in the autumn of 1916, and regained much of the ground lost. But they had suffered 542,000 casualties during the year; the Germans lost about 434,000.

1916 – The Somme

Meanwhile, Tom Wilkinson has his first experience of battle. While the French fight at Verdun, the British and a few French forces are also fighting, at the Battle of the Somme.

The sun rises red on 1st July, 1916. For a whole week Tom has crouched in the trenches while British artillery shells screamed overhead to blast the German positions in front of him. Now the time has come for the infantry to advance.

At 7.30 in the morning Tom and his friends, together with a hundred thousand other British troops, hear whistle signals from their officers. They scramble up "over the top" and form long lines in the open. More whistles signal the start of the advance. Tom begins to walk forward.

Some of the men are so confident that they kick and dribble a football in front of them. But, through the swirling smoke, Tom can see German soldiers moving in the enemy trenches not so far ahead. And German rifles are beginning to crack; machine-guns start up their deadly rattle.

Erich is one of those men in the German trenches. He has had to endure the terrible British bombardment. This is how a colleague described it: "Our dug-outs crumbled, tumbled on top of us, and our positions were razed to the ground. The 'drum-fire' [artillery bombardment] never ceased. Neither food nor water reached us. Down below, men became hysterical and their comrades had to knock them out. . ."

But Erich, and many of his German comrades, have in fact survived, and now they wait for the over-confident British. "German machine gunners and infantrymen crawled out of their holes, with inflamed and sunken eyes, their faces blackened by fire and their uniforms splashed with the blood of their wounded comrades." And then the German guns begin to fire at

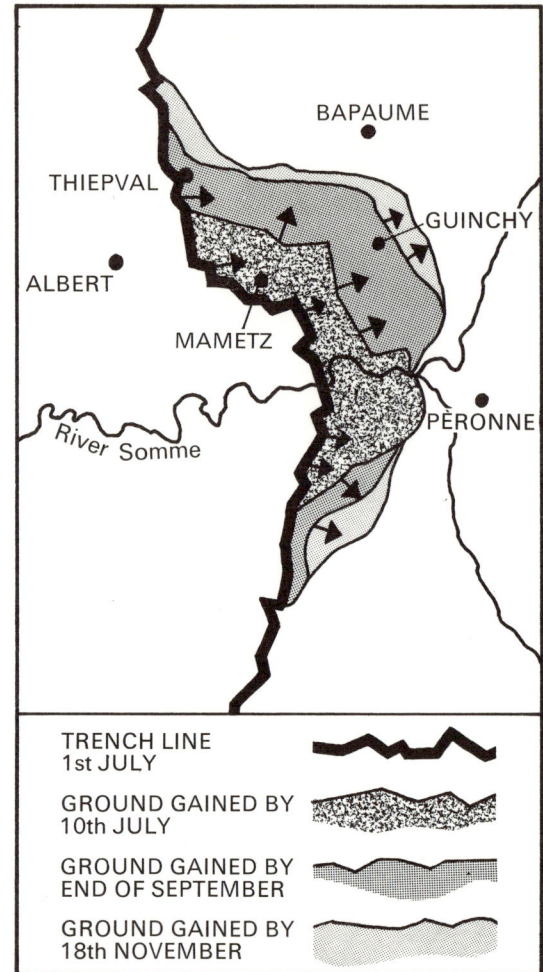

Above Plan of troop positions, and their movements, at the Battle of the Somme, 1916.

Opposite Behind the battle lines at the Somme. Wounded men lie in rows waiting for attention from the first aid teams.

58

the unprotected lines of advancing British infantrymen.

Incredibly, British troops continue to joke and sing, even as more and more of them are killed. A shell splinter zips past Tom's shoulder and severs the leg of a man just behind him.

Another wounded soldier falls, and crawls away to one side. "Lucky devil," someone calls, "You're well out of it Jimmy. Good luck to you – give 'em our love. See you later." And the advance towards death continues.

The army's worst day

This day, 1st July, 1916, would afterwards be known as the worst day in the history of the British army. Already, even Tom can see that the attack has gone disastrously wrong.

Enemy fire is steadily increasing. Machine-gun bullets sweep along the lines of advancing British troops. Tom can see row upon row of men throwing up their arms and flopping to the ground. Bullets stitch across the earth three feet in front of him, and grass chippings fly into the air, as they do from the front of a lawn mower.

The first line of British troops has reached the enemy barbed wire. They try to filter through, seeking the gaps which the artillery shells were supposed to have blown. Few of these gaps can be found and, when the troops bunch to go through, enemy machine-gun fire concentrates upon them. The gaps are soon clogged with bodies.

Tom can see other troops trying to clamber over the uncut wire. Bullets thud into them. Bodies are left stuck on the barbs. Soon the wires seem like a gigantic spider's web, with hundreds of jerking flies gummed to it.

Artillery shells thud and roar into the troops. One explodes quite close to Tom; he is thrown to the side by the blast and, when he climbs shakily to his feet again, he is confronted by all that is left of a group of four men who were hit by the shell – a boot, torn clothing, mutilated remains.

Surprisingly, Tom feels no fear. Instead there is a kind of numbness, and a fascination with all the horror around him. Almost mechanically, he continues to move forward.

But the attack has obviously failed. More and more men find shelter in dubious shell-holes. Tom does the same; and then, painfully slowly, they retreat, back to

Up and over. Troops advance across "No Man's Land" in the face of heavy enemy fire.

the British lines. By nightfall the British trenches are almost overflowing with dead and dying men.

On this one day, the British casualties topped sixty thousand, of whom nineteen thousand were dead – the greatest one-day loss ever suffered by the British army.

The offensive is continued, on and off, during the following weeks, but a major breakthrough is never achieved.

America at war

In the spring of 1917, the British and French forces received another ally. On 6th April, America declared war on Germany.

Many people in Britain thought that America's entry into the war was overdue. But the vast majority of Americans thought otherwise: they were separated from the European continent by the wide Atlantic; they were a peaceful nation; above all, they were virtually unarmed. The quarrels of Europe had little to do with them.

But, although America herself was in no immediate danger from the conflict, her ships were being attacked and sunk by German submarines. These so-called "U-boats" were attempting to strangle Britain's trade and sea supply lines. On 7th May, 1915, the liner *Lusitania* had been sunk by German submarines in the Atlantic: 1,195 people had been drowned – many of them were innocent Americans.

After this, U-boat activity had been cut back for a time. But the German naval chief, Tirpitz, protested violently. "Immediate and relentless recourse to the submarine weapon is absolutely necessary," he declared. In February 1917, the Admiral's wish was granted – Germany launched full-scale submarine attacks against enemy ships, including merchantmen, and even against neutral American vessels.

America protested strongly. But her ships continued to be attacked. And America declared war. President Wilson was not very enthusiastic. "It means," he complained, "that we shall lose our heads along with the rest."

America's entry brought great advantages to the allies – she had tremendous wealth. But she was still far from being strongly armed. Her army had to be built up; millions of men had to be recruited and trained; tanks, guns and even rifles were in short supply – some

Above The Americans enter the war. Newly arrived American troops outside a cookhouse in France, 1917.

Opposite The sinking of the *Lusitania* in 1915 by a German U-boat, with the loss of many American lives, encouraged America to join the war.

even had to come from Britain and France, despite their desperate needs.

And, although one more ally had joined the war, another was about to leave it. Russia had undergone terrible suffering. Troops and civilians began to riot. Bolshevik Communists were stirring deep unrest. Civil war, with Russians fighting against Russians, swept nearer. The Russian emperor, Tsar Nicholas II, abandoned his throne on 15th March. And, by the end of 1917, the Russians had made their separate peace with Germany.

The enemy was therefore left free to concentrate his troops in the west, in the trench zone.

1917 – Summer strain

Even before the Russians had made peace with Germany, the French army found itself unable to stand the strain of war. General Nivelle had promised victory. He had failed.

French troops rebelled against their officers. Grumbling became louder and louder. Fifty-four divisions of men refused to obey orders. Discipline collapsed. The troops would not fight, and many thousands fled from the Front.

Nivelle was replaced by Pétain, but for two weeks in May, 1917, the French army virtually ceased to defend its trenches. The Allied headquarters was in complete panic – if the Germans managed to seize this chance, the defenders would be outnumbered and terribly weak.

But Pétain managed to halt the rebellion. Discipline was gradually restored. More than ten thousand French soldiers were put on trial; 2,300 were found guilty. According to the official records, only about fifty-five were put to death, but many more probably lost their lives in secret executions.

Incredibly, the Germans never realized the full extent of this French collapse until it was too late. The British launched attacks elsewhere, to divert German attention away from the French.

Then Pétain promised to double the amount of leave given to the French troops, and improve their food. French units returned to their trenches.

But, for a time, the British had to play the leading role in attacking the Germans. The British commander, General Haig, was determined to break through the enemy lines between the North sea and the Lys River; but firstly British troops had to take the important Messines Ridge.

Careful plans were laid out by General Sir Herbert Plumer. Great quantities of shells were brought to the Front, and British artillery began a seventeen day

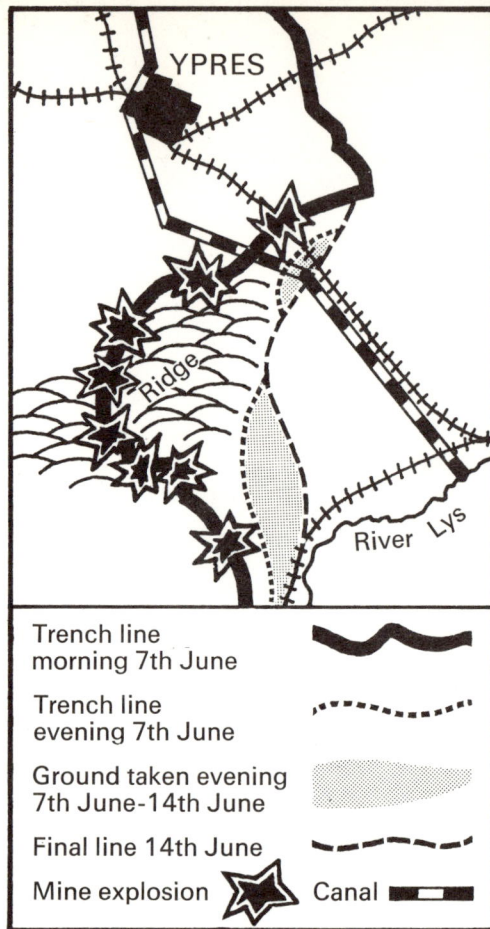

Above Plan of the Messines Ridge attack, 1917.

Trench line morning 7th June

Trench line evening 7th June

Ground taken evening 7th June–14th June

Final line 14th June

Mine explosion   Canal

Above British soldiers in possession of a German observation post on the Messines Ridge.

bombardment of the enemy positions. Mines were skilfully placed beneath the German positions on the ridge, and soon tore open a gigantic hole.

The Germans were shocked and dazed by this unexpected explosion. The British took swift advantage and leapt into the attack. Yard by yard they advanced. And, despite seventeen thousand British casualties, the Messines position was gained.

This success was looked upon as a tremendous victory. At last the Germans were being defeated. British hopes of complete victory and an end to the war were greatly boosted. Plans were quickly made for the next step forward.

Left A British patrol treads warily through the woods.

Passchendaele

We left Tom Wilkinson safely back in the British trenches after the disastrous first day of the Battle of the Somme. He survived the rest of the offensive. He was perhaps unlucky – Tom would have been better receiving some "Blighty wound" – a wound sufficient to have him sent back home.

Instead, Tom has now moved into line with the rest of his unit, ready for the next massive clash. This will later be known as the third Battle of Ypres, or Passchendaele – grim words for those who managed to survive.

Tom, in the trenches opposite Passchendaele, knows nothing of the grand plans which the British Generals have been carefully preparing. He only knows that when the whistles blow he must climb from the trench, "over the top", and walk towards the enemy machine-guns again

But he does know that a big attack is intended. Indeed, the signs are so obvious that the Germans also know it, and are making preparations accordingly to deal with it.

Rumours run riot. But, this time, Tom feels no confidence. He has learnt his lesson at the Somme: when the British artillery starts the long bombardment, Tom has little faith in the power of the shells to destroy the enemy defences.

Night after night, Tom and his friends watch the flames and flashes of the bombardment. The whole horizon seems to be lit in a massive semi-circle. The great guns discharge their shells with a noise like huge hammers pounding on iron.

The German guns reply. Tom and his friends squeeze into corners and wait for the enemy bombardment to finish. Soil and splinters shower on their helmets. Tom never knows whether the next shell might be a direct hit.

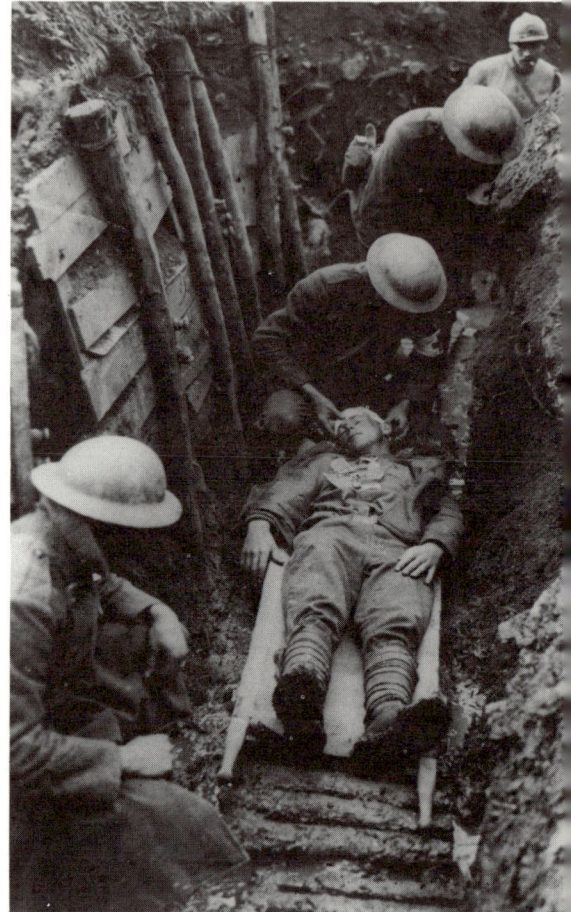

Aid to the wounded. The artillery bombardment caused many casualties. Can you see the duckboards on which the men stand, and the mud and water beneath them?

66

Waiting for the advance. Many soldiers found that having to sit it out in the trenches during an enemy bombardment was even worse than the actual attack.

So many of his friends have been killed that Tom has become used to daily additions to the list. When someone comments: "Billy bought it last night," he merely grunts. Men share out the belongings of those newly killed: Tom wears a stout pair of boots taken from one dead man, and wraps himself in a torn, stained greatcoat from another.

Mud, gas and blood

Down comes the rain. Sheets of icy storm water sluice down upon the miserable men in the trenches, drumming endlessly on helmets and groundsheets. Dug-outs and ditches overflow with black, oily flood water, and men are quite sodden, without warmth or shelter.

Shell-holes are filled with scum. The soil, broken up by the artillery barrage, is turned to sticky clinging mud.

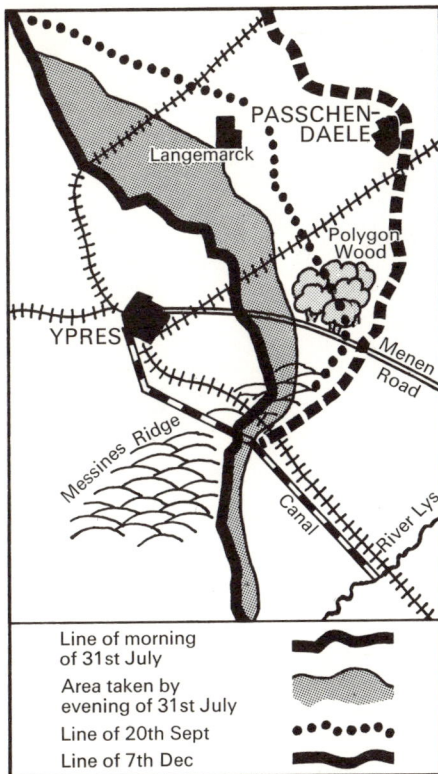

Above The area around Ypres and Passchendaele. In three and a half months, the allies gained five miles. *Opposite* Mud warfare. The sea of shell-torn mud around Passchendaele.

Line of morning of 31st July

Area taken by evening of 31st July

Line of 20th Sept

Line of 7th Dec

And now the order for the attack is given. Lines are formed; the men begin to walk forward. Again comes the enemy machine-gun fire. Again men fall in tumbled rows. The first enemy trenches are taken, but these were only lightly defended – the Germans have prepared stronger positions further back.

Tom spends the next night in one of the abandoned German trenches. Dead Germans and dead British soldiers lie indistinguishable in the mud. The rain still pours down; the artillery barrage continues, with the eerie flashing of guns lighting the black thunder clouds and the grey faces of the men.

Next morning the attack goes on. A few more yards are gained; a few more hundreds of men are slaughtered. The mud becomes thicker, and now only a few tracks are passable. And so the attack continues, day after day, week after week.

Sir Douglas Haig, the British commander, writes in one of his despatches: "The low-lying clay soil, torn up by shells and sodden with rain, turned into a succession of muddy pools. . . To leave the tracks was to risk death by drowning and, in the course of the subsequent fighting, on several occasions both men and pack animals were lost in this way."

Tom sees the remains of wounded men who, while trying to crawl back to the rear, collapsed in the mud and suffocated. The whole area is a sea of slime. Tom and his friends are coated with the black, stinking filth from head to foot – they shine and glisten like seals.

Tom, like all the ordinary soldiers, knows nothing of the overall plan of battle. He only knows about the few yards around him. There he must stay until he is ordered to do something else. His battalion is relieved, but after a brief rest he is ordered back to the hell.

Left A stretcher party struggles through the mud, Passchendaele, 1917.

69

Cavalry and tank

Haig, the British commander, was still determined to maintain pressure on the Germans even after Passchendaele. And, on 20th November, another attack was launched in front of Cambrai. And this time a new weapon was used more extensively than ever before – the tank.

Tanks, the new weapon. One of the first tanks used in the First World War abandoned on the battlefield at Ypres. Although this picture was taken in 1919, a year after the war had ended, the countryside still looks like a quagmire.

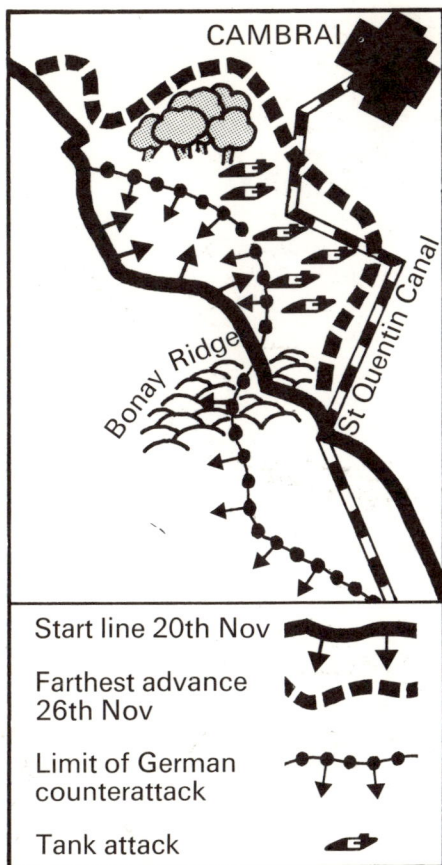

Start line 20th Nov

Farthest advance
26th Nov

Limit of German
counterattack

Tank attack

The battle of Cambrai, the first
battle in which tanks were able
to play an effective part.

The tank was the most remarkable weapon to come out of the First World War. It was developed in Britain during 1914 and 1915, after many experiments, trials and errors. Many officers, however, were strongly opposed to it – and with a certain amount of good reason. The first tanks were extremely slow and clumsy, and often broke down. Only a few people could understand that these difficulties would eventually be overcome, and that the tank was ideal for destroying enemy defences.

At the start of the war, cavalry were still considered a powerful weapon. It took a long time for some cavalry officers to realize that the machine-guns and barbed wire of trench warfare had put an end to their supremacy; cavalry could now be slaughtered as they charged.

Tanks were used at the Battle of the Somme, and during Passchendaele, but only on small scale. Now, at Cambrai, they were to be given a chance to prove what they could do. Over two hundred tanks were thrust into action. And, this time, no artillery bombardment was attempted before the battle commenced. Surprise was therefore achieved, and the ground was firmer, unscarred by shell craters.

At first, success was remarkable. The tanks charged forward on 20th November and, by four o'clock in the afternoon, the German trenches had been won for a depth of five miles across a six-mile front. Enemy defences temporarily collapsed; there even a chance of a complete breakthrough.

Many of the leading tanks however, had been put out of action – most of them through mechanical failure. Insufficient reserves could be brought up in time, and the Germans counter-attacked on 30th November and regained much of the ground lost.

But Cambrai had shown what could be done, if sufficient massed tanks were thrown into battle. Perhaps an answer had been found to the terrible trench deadlock.

Air warfare

The First World War also saw great advances in the use of the aeroplane. To Tom and his comrades it became increasingly common to see these tiny machines, whining, wheeling and diving above the trenches.

Pilots in those early days were extremely brave, and usually a little crazy too. They had to be. They tried to control frail, underpowered craft, held together only by wire, glue and good luck. Unwieldy biplanes fluttered like gigantic moths. The men had no parachutes. To be shot down meant death. The Germans joked that pilots needed a specially shaped coffin: very broad and flat. More men, though, were killed in training than in the actual fighting.

Pilots soon became heroes: the German fighter "ace" Manfred von Richtofen, known as the "Red Baron"; the deadly Englishman, Albert Ball; William Avery Bishop, the Canadian; and the French ace, Georges Marie Guynemer, who scorned manoeuvring and would plunge straight into a headlong attack.

Pilots from opposing sides behaved far better towards each other than the troops on the ground. In the early months of the war German and British pilots might fly past each other and just wave cheerily instead of shooting. This was partly because they were more bothered with flying their difficult machines than engaging in battle.

Later, this changed considerably. "Dog-fights" became vicious. The Germans invented a system whereby a machine-gun could fire between the blades of the circling propellor, thus improving the ability of the pilot to fight. Soon, all nations had adopted the idea.

But some good manners were still displayed. If a pilot was shot down behind the enemy lines, his possessions would be put into a bag and dropped over his own airfield, perhaps with a message saying that he was still alive and well.

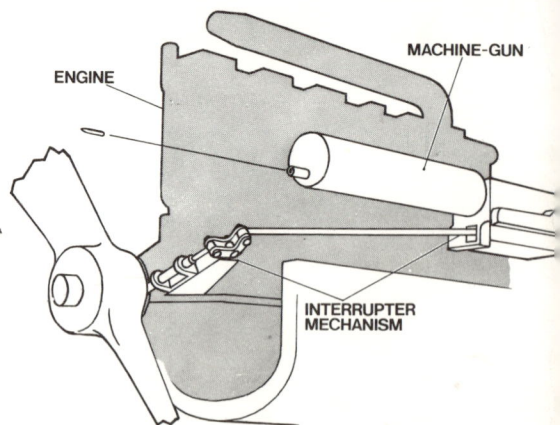

ENGINE

MACHINE-GUN

INTERRUPTER
MECHANISM

War in the air. *Above* The pilot of a Zeppelin brought down by the French and *above left* a reconnaissance squadron of eighteen British planes waiting to take off for the German lines.

Opposite The modified machine-gun mechanism which enabled pilots to fire between the blades of their aircraft's propellor.

In 1914, probably no more than two thousand aircraft existed altogether; the Americans, when they entered the war in 1917, did not have a single combat machine.

Losses were tremendous. A total of 1,300 British aircraft were used to support the troops in the second Battle of the Somme: when the fighting had ended only two hundred remained.

But warfare had been taken up into the skies, and it soon became clear that bombers and fighters could have a vital role to play.

D

The remains of an artillery post, France, 1918. Notice the devastation all around.

Victory?

As the war wore on, lessons were being learned. Tanks, used in large numbers, might be a way of breaking through the trenches. Aircraft could be a valuable weapon to support troops on the ground. Artillery bombardments did not kill as many enemy troops as expected, and instead churned up the ground, making it more difficult for the infantry and tanks to advance. These were the lessons of bitter experience. Above all, the months of terrible war had shown it to be almost impossible to advance against enemy machine-guns fired from strong defensive positions.

1918 opened with the allies still apparently far from victory. Attacks in western Europe had bogged down. Russia had collapsed. German U-boats were still sinking essential supplies to Britain.

Yet time was now on the allied side. The Germans realized that if they did not win quickly, growing American strength might prove too much for them. Germany was also suffering from exhaustion and short supplies; this exhaustion might soon be crippling. The German military leader, Ludendorff, therefore planned for a massive, all-out attack. Preparations were made secretly throughout the dark winter months.

More German troops were now available for the trenches, since the Russians front had collapsed. Units were rushed over from the east. In France and Britain, on the other hand, men were already increasingly scarce: so many of them had been slaughtered.

The British and French scanned the countryside, seeking out all available men. Soon there would be no-one left to recruit.

Ludendorff hoped to smash the allied armies through a series of huge hammer blows. He wanted to drive a deep wedge between the British and the French forces. His plans were completed by March, 1918. Germany's last attempt was about to begin.

Germany's last attack

Although Germany had been slow to build tanks, she had found another answer to the trench stalemate. Instead of pushing solid lines of men into the slaughter, the German commander, Ludendorff, decided to use specially-trained "shock troops": these would filter forward under artillery cover, and would then pierce the enemy's defences at a number of selected weak points.

This was what happened when the giant German offensive opened on 21st March, 1918. The shock troops dashed forward in thick fog, slashing into the British lines along a sixty mile front. Unlike previous attacks, they left the strongest British positions well alone, to be dealt with by more troops coming up behind.

The area held by the British Fifth Army collapsed. All reserves were rushed forward in an attempt to plug the gap.

On 12th April, General Haig issued his famous "Backs to the Wall" order, forbidding retreat. This is how it read: "Many amongst us now are tired. To those I would say that Victory will belong to the side

Above The last year of the war. Much needed reinforcements arriving from America.

Opposite German storm troopers advance through woods to attack the French lines. Notice how they are wearing gas masks, in case of a gas attack.

Top right Germany's answer to the trench stalemate was to use specially-trained shock troops to attack the enemy's weak points.

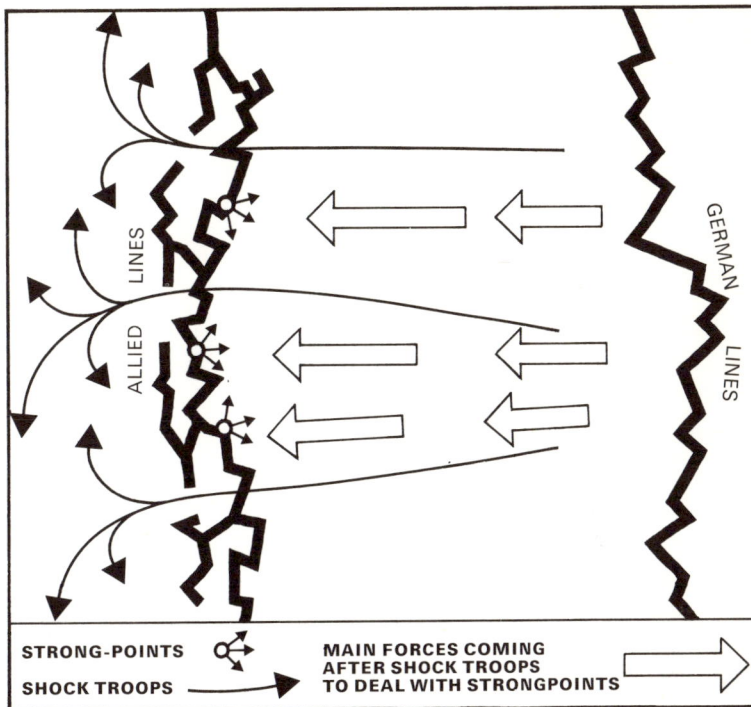

STRONG-POINTS

SHOCK TROOPS

MAIN FORCES COMING
AFTER SHOCK TROOPS
TO DEAL WITH STRONGPOINTS

which holds out the longest . . . There is no other course open to us but to fight it out."

And fight it out the British did. Desperately, they clung to their positions. Equally desperately, the Germans clawed forward. But once again the Germans were halted, on 17th April.

Ludendorff tried once more, on 27th May. He struck at the French along the Chemin des Dames. The French collapsed. Again all troops, including Americans, were pushed into the defence, and, in June, the Germans were checked at the battles of Chateau-Thierry and Belleau Wood.

A deep dent had been driven into the allied positions. Ludendorff tried to take advantage of this by further attacks in June and July, but failed. In five months he had lost half a million men. Allied losses had been even greater, but American troops were now arriving at a rate of 300,000 a month. And the British, French and Americans were preparing to hit back.

Approaching climax

The allies counter-attacked on 18th July in the area of the Marne, with American troops playing a leading role. In a series of devastating assaults, the Germans were hurled back all along the line, despite brave resistance.

Ludendorff's attempts to crush the remaining allied opposition had failed. His losses were crippling – three thousand machine-guns alone. British, French and American hopes soared. The sweet smell of victory began to scent the air. The Germans, on the other hand, were plunged into black despair.

The allies kept up the pressure with an offensive at Amiens, starting on 8th August. Once again the value of tanks was clearly shown: plans for the attack were kept strictly secret, and the Germans were quite

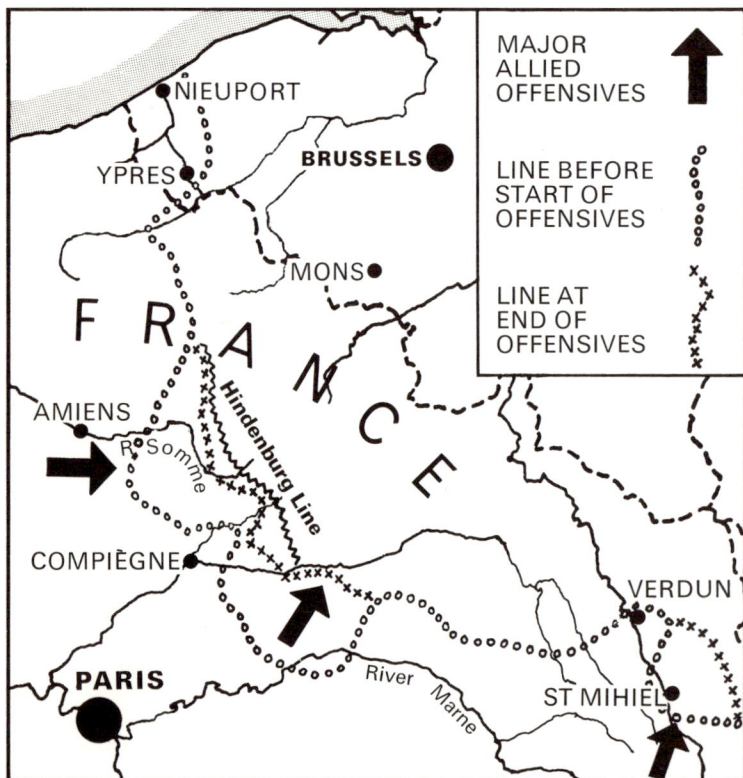

Left Map of northern France showing the positions of the opposing armies at the time of the final offensives in 1918.

unprepared. Nor was any artillery bombardment carried out before the British tanks rolled forward. Canadian, Australian and New Zealand troops waded into the fight, helped by dense fog. Over fifteen thousand enemy prisoners were taken.

The attacks continued between 21st August and 4th September, as the Allied troops pushed relentlessly forward; step by step, the Germans were forced to give ground.

Commonwealth troops crossed the Somme on 30th August, and Canadian forces broke through the enemy lines on 2nd September. The German situation worsened. Valuable equipment had to be left behind in the churned-up mud of the battlefields: vehicles, guns, ammunition. German troops collapsed from exhaustion; many went mad in the panic and misery of continuous shell-fire and retreat.

The German army soon had to withdraw to its final position on the Hindenburg Line. The allies had taken at least thirty thousand prisoners. And Ludendorff realized that the end could not be far away. He moaned: "This war must be ended."

The Americans then proved that there was no hope left for the Germans, by attacking the important area around St. Mihiel on 12th September. Troops were supported by about six hundred aircraft – American, French, Italian and Portuguese. The Germans were cleared from the area by 16th September – leaving fifteen thousand prisoners behind. This had been the largest American operation since the U.S. Civil War, and American troops had shown themselves to be formidable fighters.

Top American troops crossing a pontoon bridge over the river Marne.
Above American soldiers on guard over German prisoners.

Defeat

Foch, the supreme Allied commander, planned a number of attacks on the final German positions. These thrusts would, he hoped, shatter the German forces completely.

The attacks began on 26th September in the Meuse-Argonne area. American and French units thrust against the thickly defended Argonne Forest and, although the Germans rushed in reinforcements, by

Map of the final allied attack against the German positions, September, 1918.

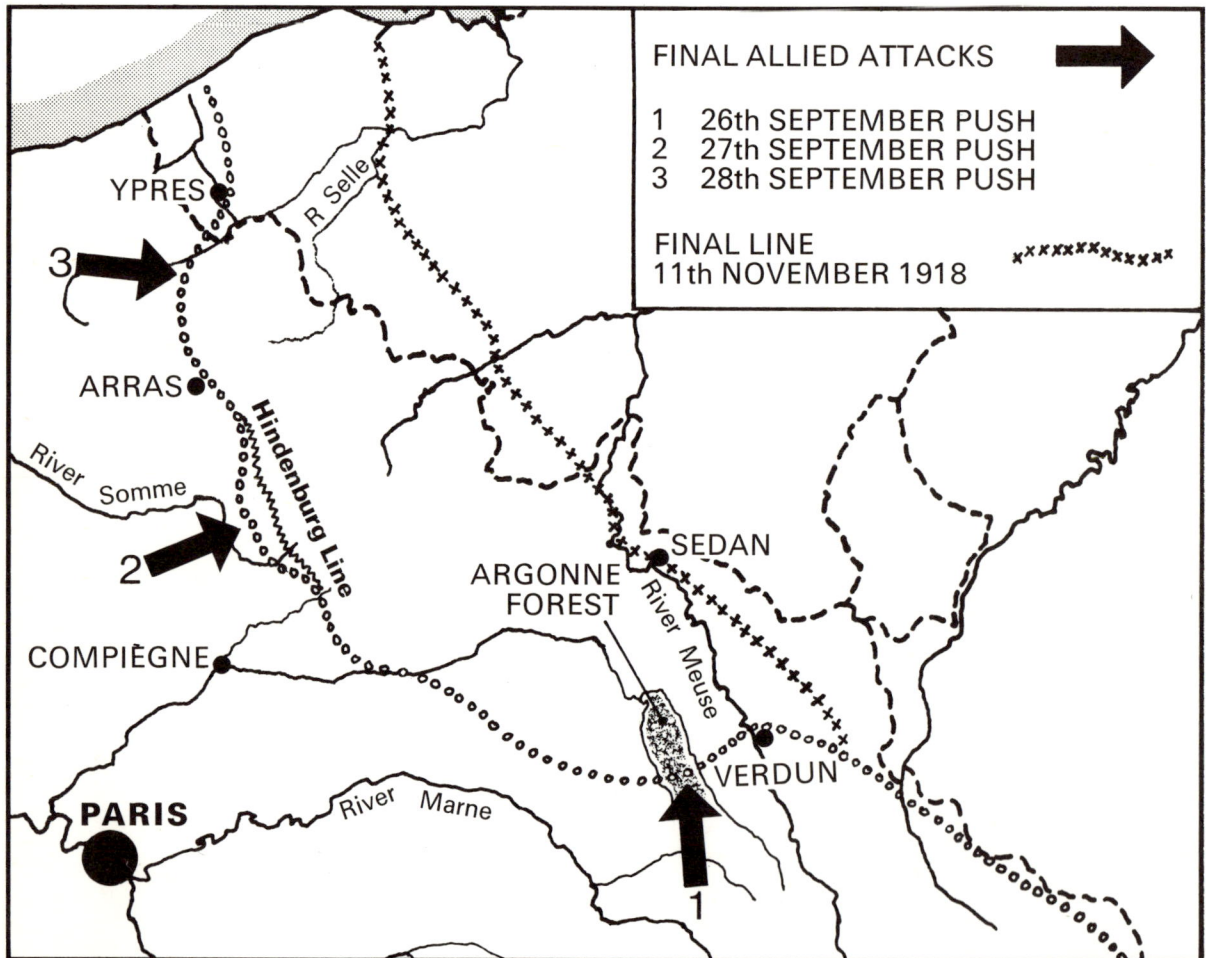

YPRES

R. Selle

ARRAS

River Somme

Hindenburg Line

COMPIÈGNE

PARIS

River Marne

ARGONNE FOREST

SEDAN

River Meuse

VERDUN

FINAL ALLIED ATTACKS

1 26th SEPTEMBER PUSH
2 27th SEPTEMBER PUSH
3 28th SEPTEMBER PUSH

FINAL LINE
11th NOVEMBER 1918

The end of the First World War.
Leaders pose for photographs after
signing the Armistice, in a railway
carriage near Compiègne, on 11th
November, 1918.

3rd October the Americans had cut through the first and second German defence lines.

Progress slowed down in the face of stubborn German resistance. American troops had to batter their way forward, losing many men in frontal attacks. But, by the end of October, the American First Army had forced its way through most of the third and final German line. Tired divisions were replaced by fresh troops for the next, decisive push. The German defences were shattered.

Meanwhile, on 27th September, the British army had attacked further north, against the Hindenburg Line. The Germans put up incredible resistance, and, although forced to pull back, they managed to prevent the British from breaking through completely.

British–Belgian troops in Flanders received a similar setback. They swept over the Ypres Ridge, but were then forced to slow down: supply problems were great, and the Germans fought back bravely.

But, because of the American and French progress in the Meuse–Argonne–Sedan area, Ludendorff had to order a general German retreat. The war was now clearly lost, although the German leaders still hoped to hang on until winter.

This hope soon faded. The British Fourth Army, under Rawlinson, smashed through German defences on the Selle River on 17th October; the British Third Army crossed lower down on 20th October; and the combined British and Belgian armies began to move forward again in Flanders.

German resistance started to crack up under this terrible pressure. Ludendorff resigned; the German Fleet mutinied; disorders, riots and rebellions broke out inside Germany. A new government took office. The Germans, at last, sued for peace.

Talks took place in a railway carriage in a forest at Compiègne, near Paris. Agreement was finally reached at five o'clock in the morning on 11th November, 1918. Six hours later, the incessant firing ceased at last.

Why did the Germans lose?

On 11th November, 1918, the day the "Great War" ended, the German army remained battered and bloody, but not yet broken. The German forces had not even been driven back into their own country. They still remained on French soil. The British army had in fact only managed to struggle back to where it

The arrival of increasing numbers of American troop reinforcements did much to ensure the defeat of Germany.

had started in 1914. Yet the Germans had clearly lost the war, and asked for peace. Why?

The Germans had made three great mistakes during the war. Their first mistake was to march through Belgium in 1914. This was bound to bring in Belgium's ally, Britain, although many people in Britain never wanted to go to war with Germany.

Secondly, the Germans did not try hard enough to keep the Americans out of the war. They had even less of a quarrel with America than they had with Britain, and many Americans were very reluctant indeed to fight in this "foreign conflict" which had nothing to do with them.

But German submarines sank American ships; innocent American lives were lost; stern speeches were made. This allowed those few people in America who did want to join in the struggle to collect popular support.

And, once the Americans were in, the result was almost certain to be a German defeat. The United States had vast supplies of manpower and materials, far greater than the Germans could ever achieve. Germany fast became exhausted; so too did Britain and France – but they could be boosted by America.

The third mistake the Germans made was, strangely enough, to continue to fight so hard in 1918. At the end of 1917, the allies were tired and depressed; the Americans had still not arrived in any great strength, and the Germans, although also weary, held strong positions.

Had the Germans merely strengthened these positions, stayed on the defensive, and then sought peace, the allies would have been prepared to listen. They would also have given more away in the peace talks, in order to save lives.

Instead, the Germans attacked. This weakened them. The allies could then strike back, greatly aided by newly-arrived American support. And, when peace eventually came, they could make strict demands.

Victory

Tom Wilkinson has survived the war. He is now twenty-one. War in the trenches has made him old beyond his years. He has been to hell, and he has returned.

Tom survives, but he will never be the same again. His hands shake, and sometimes he can scarcely control them. He has a rasping cough, which he will

The war is over. A London street on 11th November as news of the Armistice spreads.

A London bus crowded with people celebrating the end of the war.

never lose. He has frequent nightmares.

During those days of terrible battle, when he allowed himself to think of peace, he thought that he would be happy then beyond his wildest dreams. Now, like thousands of others like him, he finds the reality quite different.

The numbness continues, the same dull feeling which he had in battle and in the terror of the trenches. He reaches London, and sees the joyful crowds of civilians. Banners stream from buildings, brass bands thump and echo through the jammed streets, people dance and sing outside – but Tom feels set apart from it all. Other soldiers feel the same.

Only when Tom reaches home, only when he walks in the fields and hears the birds sing in the country-side – only then will the tide of peace begin to soothe him.

Meanwhile, in London, Paris, New York, and in towns and villages throughout the victorious nations, celebrations continue.

All work in Britain stopped for the day on 11th November. Factories stood empty. People were in the streets instead, and they seemed almost drunk.

Celebrations continued in London for two more days. People started smashing shop windows – just for the fun of it. Vehicles were overturned, and some were set on fire. In the end, the police had to clear the streets and drag some of the rowdiest people off to the cells.

Paris was quieter after the first day. Civilians in France, like the soldiers, were still too shocked and numbed by the horror of it all.

Berlin was nearly as rowdy as London, but for a different reason. Civil war had almost broken out in the disaster of defeat. Erich and other returning soldiers found barricades in the Berlin streets; they could hear the crack of rifles and the thump of mortars. Some troops survived the war only to be shot down in their own city by fellow-Germans.

The price

Germany was paying the price of defeat. But all nations, whether winners or losers, had a price to pay.

As each day passed, Tom found yet another friend had been killed, or was missing, or terribly wounded. In his street there was scarcely a single family which

The human cost of the war – a mass burial of some of the victims. But for most of the eight and a half million men who died there was no grave and no burial.

had not lost a father, a son or some close relation.

Erich, the German soldier, had the same experience. Most of the boys he knew at school were dead; most of their bodies would never be found.

And Erich experienced another side of the war. His wounded leg was healing, but he remained in a crowded hospital in Berlin. And in this hospital with him were the victims of shell-shock – men whose minds had been shattered by the blast of explosion and the strain of fear.

They were kept in special wards, which sometimes had soft padded walls to prevent the patients from hurting themselves. These men still suffered the thoughts and fears of battle, even though the battles had long since ended.

Some kept their faces covered with their hands, to protect themselves from shell-splinters, even though these splinters had long since ceased to fly. They would not remove their hands, even to eat. Other men hid their heads in blankets, and cried like babies when anyone tried to remove the covering. Others just sat, and silently wept.

This was part of the price of war. And British soldiers suffered these same waking nightmares. Win or lose, the same damage had been done. Ordinary men, British, French, Belgian, American or German, had been turned into killers and into victims.

One German wrote after his first battle: "Of my group of eight, two had been killed. One of the others was a chimney sweep, two were farmers, one a student and another a teacher – all ordinary peace-loving people who, a few months ago, would not have harmed anyone.

"Now they told each other what they had achieved; one had killed a Frenchman with a pickaxe, another had strangled an officer, and a third had crushed the skull of a Frenchman with his rifle. Now we are all murderers."

Conclusion

Strangely enough, there was no hate between the opposing soldiers during the war, except perhaps in the blind fury of battle. At Christmas in 1914, German and British troops met between their trenches, shook hands, swopped badges and took each other's photographs before they were all ordered back into their trenches to kill one another again.

Often, if British and German soldiers were out in front of their trenches laying barbed wire, neither side would shoot at the other until the wire-work had been completed. At other times, a short pause might come in the fighting, to allow the wounded to be collected.

One British soldier wrote home from the trenches: "I respect the Germans as soldiers. I sympathize with the poor devil of a German infantryman who goes through the same hell as I do."

Such feelings increased the stupidity of the slaughter. The war was senseless from beginning to end. Nobody really wanted it to start. Nobody really won it. The price of victory was almost as great as the price of defeat. And the same problems remained after the Treaty of Versailles, which officially ended the war, as had existed in 1914.

In 1918, both victors and defeated lay bleeding and exhausted. Yet nothing had been solved. Germany still felt threatened by France. France still felt threatened by Germany. The "balance of power" had still to be maintained.

All those millions of men had gone to war, most of them unwillingly; all those millions of men had been slaughtered; and the only gain was a few useless yards of ground.

Survivors went home; the dead remained. The battlefields fell silent, apart from the dripping water in the deserted trenches. Mud scarred the earth, and where once grass had grown, now small white crosses

stretched neatly across the landscape.

"A war to end all wars" – this had been the pious hope. But the next World War was only twenty years away.

The war poet Siegfried Sassoon wrote about it:

"Do you remember the rats; and the stench
Of corpses rotting in front of the front-line trench.
And dawn coming, dirty-white, and chill with a
    hopeless rain?
Do you ever stop and ask, 'Is it going to happen again?'"

The material cost of the war. A French soldier surveys Arras Cathedral, shattered by the German bombardment. But the "war to end all wars" was not the end of war; twenty-one years later, another still more devastating war was to be declared.

Table of Dates

1914

28th June	Archduke Franz Ferdinand assassinated at Sarajevo.
25th July	Austria declares war on Serbia.
1st August	German troops enter Belgium; Britain declares war on Germany.
10th August	First units of the B.E.F. arrive in France.
23rd August	Battle of Mons – the allies retreat.
30th October	First Battle of Ypres – the B.E.F. virtually wiped out.

1915

22nd April	Second Battle of Ypres; deadlock.
7th May	The sinking of the *Lusitania*.
6th August	The start of the Gallipoli operation.
25th September	Battle of Loos – massive British casualties.
19th September	Haig made British Commander-in-Chief.

1916

21st January	Battle of Verdun – stubborn defence by the French.
May–June	Arrival of Kitchener's Army in France.
31st May	Naval battle of Jutland.
1st July	First Battle of the Somme – the worst day in the history of the British army.
29th August	Hindenburg made German Chief-of-Staff.
6th December	Lloyd George becomes British Prime Minister.

1917

1st February	Germany starts unrestricted submarine warfare.
15th March	Russian Tsar abdicates.
6th April	America declares war on Germany.
1st August	Third Battle of Ypres (Passchendaele) – British troops attack through a sea of mud.
20th November	Battle of Cambrai; tanks used successfully for the first time.
15th December	Russian–German peace treaty signed at Brest-Litovsk. Germany free now to concentrate on the Western Front.

1918

21st March	German offensive begins, using specially-trained shock troops.
18th July	Second Battle of the Marne at which American troops play a leading role.
8th August	British tanks break through at Amiens.
27th September	Hindenburg Line broken; German defences almost shattered.
28th October	German commander Ludendorff resigns.
29th October	German fleet mutinies.
9th November	German Kaiser abdicates.
11th November	Armistice signed in a railway carriage near Compiègne. The firing ceases.

Glossary

ALLIES   Countries which have united to fight in a common cause.

BATTALION   An infantry unit composed of three or four companies and forming part of a regiment or brigade.

BAYONET   A short steel blade attached to the muzzle of a rifle and used for stabbing at close quarters.

B.E.F.   British Expeditionary Force; a small but highly trained British army which fought in France in 1914.

BIPLANE   An early form of aeroplane which had two parallel wings at each side.

BLIGHTY   The nickname used by the soldiers to describe England, or home.

BREAST-WORK   A low parapet of earth, designed to protect the front of a trench from enemy attack and sniper fire.

BREECH   The rear part of a gun-barrel, into which the ammunition is loaded.

COMPANY   A division of an infantry battalion.

CONSCRIPTION   The compulsory enrolment of men into the armed forces.

CORDITE   A smokeless explosive powder, introduced in 1891.

DIVISION   A large section of an army, under the command of a Major General; usually consisting of three infantry brigades of about 10,000 to 15,000 men.

DUG-OUT   An underground shelter which has been dug into the ground.

FIRE-STEP   A ledge in a trench on which soldiers stood to fire over the top of the breast-work.

FLANK   One side of an army or group of soldiers.

GRENADE   A small explosive shell thrown by hand.

MAGAZINE   A container into which bullets are fitted for continuous firing; also a storehouse for explosives, ammunition and weapons.

MOBILIZE   To gather and prepare armed forces for active service.

MUZZLE   The end of the barrel of a gun from which the bullets emerge; the mouth of the gun.

NO MAN'S LAND   The ground between two rows of opposing trenches.

PLATOON   A subdivision of an infantry company; usually commanded by a lieutenant.

PROPAGANDA   Biased information intended to convert people to a particular point of view.

REFUGEE   Someone who flees to a foreign country to seek safety from war or hardship.

REGIMENT   A permanent unit of an army, divided into battalions.

SALIENT   A trench position which protruded out into enemy territory.

SAP   A trench dug deep underground for approaching and undermining enemy positions.

SECTION   A subdivision of an infantry platoon.

TRENCH   A deep ditch used by the soldiers for cover, and as living quarters.

ULTIMATUM   A final demand or proposal of terms, the rejection of which usually leads directly to conflict.

Further Reading

Barnett, Correlli, *The Sword Bearers* (Penguin, 1966) – portraits of the leading generals.

Blunden, Edmund, *Undertones of War* (Cobden Sanderson, 1929) – a distinguished poet describes his terrible experiences in the trenches.

Farrar-Hockley, Antony, *The Somme* (Pan Books, 1970) – the drama and the terror of the dreadful Somme fighting.

Gardner, Brian (ed.) *Up the Line to Death* (Methuen, 1964) – a collection of war poetry, with a foreword by Edmund Blunden, full of pity, fear and horror.

Graves, Robert, *Goodbye to all That* (Penguin, 1969) – a magnificent picture of the roots of the fighting.

Haigh, R. H. and Turner, P. W., *Not for Glory* (Maxwell, 1969) – the story of one man's war, an ordinary North Country boy thrown into the conflict.

Parkinson, Roger, *The Origins of World War One* (Wayland, 1970) – the reasons for the war, and the events leading up to it, are illustrated by contemporary documents.

Remarque, Erich Maria, *All Quiet on the Western Front* (Mayflower, 1968) – perhaps the best war novel ever written, revealing the agony of an ordinary soldier fighting on the German side.

Taylor, A. J. P., *The First World War* (Penguin, 1970) – a pictorial history of the war; the photographs say more than words ever could.

Index

Picture Credits

The Publishers wish to thank the following for their kind permission to reproduce copyright illustrations on the pages mentioned: Popperfoto, *frontispiece*, 8, 13, 18–19, 25, 38, 45, 46 (bottom), 48, 49, 50–51, 51, 53, 54, 59, 64–65, 65, 68, 68–69, 76 (bottom), 81, 88–89; Paramount Pictures, 82; the Radio Times Hulton Picture Library, 10, 27, 29, 30, 32 (top), 34, 34–35, 40–41, 41, 42, 42–43, 46–47 (top), 56–57, 60–61, 62–63 (top), 66, 67, 70, 73, 74, 76–77 (top), 78–79 (top and bottom), 84, 85, 86; the Mansell Collection, 14, 16, 20–21, 22, 26, 28, 32 (bottom), 37, 63 (bottom), 72. Other illustrations appearing in this book are the property of the Wayland Picture Library.

Drawings and design by Grout, Fry and Associates.